"The modern state of ~~Israel~~ is one of the ~~Jews~~' brief success stories, but this must be the last. 80*

Islam, Christianity,
and
The State of Israel

as fulfillment of Old Testament prophecy

By Dr. Ahmad Shafaat

—theme: ii, 16, 30, 40, 46, 69-70, 73,

— Christians have no hope of salvation 32
(cf Morey p.202 = a hadith on this)
— Christianity is unreasonable — 57, 60,

NOTE: How Islam depends upon ① an original theory of "textual erosion" and uses as an ally the 19thc. academic Euro— — 10, 19f, version ② evolutionary theory 22-23 of religious advance — 10, N.4

ISBN. 0-89259-082-3

Dedicated to my father, Abdur Rahman Khan

About the Author

Dr. Ahmad Shafaat (b. 1943) hails from Lahore (Pakistan), where he studied Islam under the renowned Islamic scholar Ahmad Ali. He won his Ph.D. (Math) in 1968, and thereafter taught Mathematics and Business Statistics in various Canadian Universities and in King Abdulaziz University, Jeddah, Saudi Arabia. He has published over 25 research articles in Mathematics. Later from 1979 to 1981 he pursued some research on Christian-Muslim relations at the Islamic Foundation, Leicester, U.K. Some of his works published so far include the following:

1. The Gospel According to Islam
2. The Question of The Authenticity and the Authority of the Bible
3. The Concept of God (In Missionary Christianity and Islam)
4. Islam and Its Prophet: A Fulfillment of Biblical Prophecies

Currently he is resident in Canada and edits an Islamic Magazine "Al-Ummah." He is also a founder of a Society for Islamic Unity.

Contents

Introduction

Perhaps no pre-Christian tradition has had such prolonged and extensive influence in history as the MESSIANIC tradition that finds expression in both the Old Testament and subsequent Jewish writings. Christianity, with its tremendous influence in the past twenty centuries, and now comprising one-fifth of mankind, was originally inspired by that tradition; what is generally not known is that Islam, an even more influential religious movement, also relates with that tradition, though it cannot in any sense be said to be inspired by it.

The influence of the messianic tradition is a continuing one. In our times, the creation of the State of Israel, which is clearly an event of far-reaching political significance for the entire world, was directly inspired by Old Testament messianic promises that one day all Jews would return to the land of Palestine and re-establish a kingdom ruled by the descendants of David. In the Christian world new sects continue to emerge on the basis of claims that the Old Testament messianic prophecies, as understood by Christians, will soon find their final and complete fulfillment in the second coming of Jesus. The Jehovah's Witnesses, Mormons, and Moonies are examples of such sects.

As widely circulated predictions about the future made in the ancient past, Jewish messianic writings acquire influential authority to suggest and support a social or political course of action in the present, especially in times when men have extreme difficulty finding fulfillment by conceiving unaided and actualizing a vision of a better future. The course of action suggested and supported by messianic expectations can be very positive. Jesus used these expectations to revive his people's spirit and lead them to true religious commitment.

Sometimes, however, messianic expectations can inspire futile and even dangerous developments. Many Christian sects have originated in the expectant hope that the end of the world is imminent and that Jesus will soon return. Such expectations have so far always proved false and have resulted only in the creation of small sects desperate for converts and serving little purpose in the Christian church or the world at large. More harmful manifestations of Christian messianism are possible in the future. Imagine for a moment that, instead of inspiring obscure small sects, the expectation of the last days and the return of Jesus were to grip a significant portion of the Christian population of the world (even 12 per cent of the total Christian population would amount to more than 100 million people) and that a man lusting for glory were to succeed in convincing them that he was the returned Jesus. Since the New Testament teaches (Luke 19:27, II Thess. 1:7-8 and Apoc. 19:11-6) that Jesus will return as the powerful and glorious ruler of the whole world who will judge and punish all who reject God and the good news, this person claiming to be the returned Jesus might distort this Revelation and do everything possible, with the help of his millions of followers and all the organizational and technological skills available in his time, to wage a war of genocide against all non-Christians. Needless to say, the results would be disastrous.

If this possibility seems remote, the disastrous results of another attempt to fulfill messianic predictions are available for all to see. A planned Jewish effort to fulfill a section of Old Testament messianic prophecies, based on the secular distortion of a spiritual message, has led to the creation of the State of Israel and has seriously compromised the principles of justice common to all three of the Abrahamic or revealed religions and created a great deal of economic and political instability in the world. It has the potential even to become the main cause of a destructive global war.

The potential of messianic prophecies to inspire far-reaching developments that can at times adversely affect the whole of mankind makes these prophecies an important subject, deserving attention by Muslims and a fresh and honest assessment by Jews and Christians.

These prophecies become dangerous only when they are interpreted too literally as predictions of future events or when men make forced efforts to bring about those events instead of leaving their fulfillment to God, to Whom it belongs (cf. Mark 4:26-29). Most of the messianic prophecies were originally construed as hopes or warnings, not as predictions or as serious claims to a genuine knowledge of the future. Even

[ii]

if such knowledge is implicitly or explicitly claimed, the prophecies in the form that has survived in the most authoritative Jewish book, the Old Testament, are suspect, because many such prophecies have been proven to be false or are clearly contradictory (see Chapter II below). To construct a concrete picture of the future world out of such prophecies centuries after they were written down and millennia after they were revealed and then try to turn such a picture into reality is to put them to a use for which they were never intended.

But what then, if any, is the value of these prophecies? The messianic prophecies derive their value primarily from the historical perspective of revelation. They represent a stage and a form of revelation intended to teach certain religious principles, such as the unity and transcendence of God and the principle that God is the real king, that God is righteous, and that, despite the fact that His people may seem to suffer in the present, His justice will not allow the destiny of the righteous to be the same as, or worse than that of the wicked. The predictive form of the messianic prophecy underlines the fact that the complete manifestation of God's justice must be seen in the future, for the present seems to distribute suffering without strict regard for people's ethical and moral behavior.

With the messianic prophecy thus understood as a form and a stage in the history of revelation, and specifically of the most fundamental principles of religion, its "fulfillment" primarily means the development of these principles to their ultimate stage and their victory in history. It is in this sense that Christianity and Islam "fulfill" messianic prophecy. Through Islam, with Christianity playing a preparatory role, the religious principles enshrined in the messianic prophecies find their complete development and achieve worldwide acceptance. In doing this, Islam and Christianity have also inspired developments in history that have impressive correspondence with some of the messianic predictions, although we regard this as due largely to the fact that the logic behind these predictions was especially sound, not because the composers of these predictions could in every case foresee these developments centuries before they took place.

The present book considers the messianic prophecies and their fulfillment in the above light. These prophecies are regarded as a form and stage of revelation and their "fulfillment" as primarily the completion of that revelation. This book is a kind of history of Judeo-Christian-Islamic revelation, with the influential subject of messianic prophecies providing the central theme. We shall concentrate on prophecies in the

Old Testament, which is the most basic and the only collection of religious books universally recognized by Jews as authentic revelation. It is hoped that this book will strengthen the religious principles revealed in the messianic prophecies and developed in subsequent revelations and thereby will discourage artificial and disastrous attempts to use messianism as a means to interfere with the natural course of history.

A few points about the presentation in the book should be noted here. Translations of Biblical passages are taken from the King James version, except where modern scholarship has shown these to be inaccurate or where their meaning needs to be clarified. Pronouns referring to Yahweh, the god of Israel, are capitalized when He is not conceived as a national deity but conceived rather in universal, monotheistic, and transcendent terms. The title "prophet" is used for Biblical personalities without implying that they either were or were not "true" prophets; for example, if we speak of the prophet Ezekiel we, by this use of the title alone, imply nothing about whether he was truly inspired by God or not.

Statements about Israelite or Biblical traditions are not meant to be statements about the authentic divine revelations received by Israelites or Biblical prophets. For example, it if is stated that in the Biblical tradition true monotheism did not find full expression until Second Isaiah, this does not mean that true monotheism was not preached by true prophets who lived before the time of Second Isaiah.

The author prays for the blessings and peace of Allah (SWT)* on the Prophet Muhammad (SAWS), Jesus Christ (AS), John the Baptist (AS) and all the true prophets who passed away before them.

*Abbreviations used in this book:
SWT = subhanahu wa t'ala (glorification of Allah)
SAWS = sall-allahu alayhi wa sallam (blessings on Prophet Muhammad)
AS = alayhi as-salam (blessings on a true prophet of God)

Chapter I

Historical Development of Messianic Prophecy: A Summary

T he primary concern in this present book is the fulfillment of messianic prophecy and not the messianic prophecy in itself. Therefore we shall content ourselves here with only a brief sketch of the developments of messianic prophecy, and will not discuss in detail the various questions involved, although such detailed discussion by other scholars[1] has been taken into account.

The Ideal of Kingship

The ground for the building of messianic ideas was provided by the nationalistic aspirations of the Israelites in the time of their earlier kings. The religious spirit responsible for the unique development of these ideas was provided mainly by monotheistic tendencies in the Israelites' conception of God. The nationalistic aspirations of the Israelites, like those of other nations, were expressed as an ideal of kingship and as ideal hopes and expectations about the character of the reigning king and the conditions that prevailed in his reign. We can get an idea of the Israelites' ideal of kingship from the Psalms, some of which were read at the ceremony of the anointing of a king or his annual enthronement at the New Year's Festival or other such official occasion.

The king and his princes were expected to rule with divine justice and righteousness and to bring extraordinary prosperity. In a Psalm traditionally ascribed to Solomon, the king or the priest prays thus at a ceremony:

> Give the king thy judgments, O God, and thy righteousness unto the king's son;
> That he may judge thy people with righteousness, and thy poor with judgment.
> The mountains may bring peace to the people, and the little hills righteousness.

> Let him judge the poor of the people, let him save the children
> of the needy and break in pieces the oppressor . . .
> . . . He shall come down like rain upon the mown grass, as showers
> that water the earth . . .
> . . . There shall be a handful (plenty) of corn in the earth, (even)
> upon the top of the mountains;
> The fruit thereof shall shake like Lebanon and they of the city shall
> flourish like grass of the earth.
>
> (Psalm 72:1-4, 6, 16)

The king on the throne is also expected to defeat all the nation's
enemies and rule the world:

> He shall have dominion also from sea to sea, and from the river
> unto the ends of the earth.
> They that dwell in the wilderness shall bow before him, and his
> enemies shall lick the dust.
>
> (Psalm 72:8-9)

The Israelite kingdom, founded by David, is expected to last for ever:

> For thy servant David's sake turn not away the face of thine
> anointed (i.e. the reigning king who sits on David's throne).
> The Lord hath sworn in truth unto David; He will not turn from
> it; of the fruit of thy body (of thy offspring, O David) will I set upon
> thine throne.
> If thy children will keep my covenant and my testimony that I
> shall teach them, their children shall also sit upon thine throne for
> evermore.
>
> (Psalm 132:10-12)

The choice of the king is believed to have been made by Israel's God,
Yahweh. That is why the king is called "Yahweh's" or "thine anointed
(or messiah)" in the above passage, an expression which means that it
is Yahweh who has made the king's appointment. The king sitting on
his throne is pictured sitting on the right hand of God:

> Yahweh said to my lord (the king):
> Sit thou at my right hand until I make thine enemies thy footstool.
> Yahweh shall send the rod of thy strength out of Zion; rule then
> in the midst of thine enemies.
>
> (Psalm 110:1-2)

The king can be called a son of God (Psalm 89:27, 1 Chronicles 22:10).

This picture of Israelite kingship agrees with the way other nations in the near east viewed their institution of kingship. The Babylonian, Assyrian, and Egyptian kings, too, are sons of God or gods. They are chosen by the gods to make right shine in the country. They bring comfort and joy to the downtrodden and defeat the oppressors. The gods send down rain and other blessings and there is peace and prosperity.

A text on the enthronement of Rameses IV reads:

O happy day: Heaven and earth rejoice,
for thou art the great lord of Egypt.
They that hungered are satisfied and happy,
they that thirsted are drunken. . . .
They that were naked are clad in fine linen . . .
They that were in prison are set free . . . .
They that were in uproar in this land are at peace.

In an Assyrain text, a courtier writes about the king:

The gods Shamash and Adad have granted the king:
a gracious reign, orderly days,
years of righteousness,
abundant rains, copious inundations, acceptable prices.
Old men dance, young men sing,
matrons, maidens are gay with laughter . . .

A text on Ashurbanipal's accession to the throne reads:

Adad sent down his showers,
He opened his fountains,
The corn grew five ells high in its ear;
The spike became five sixths of an ell.

A hymn from the enthronement of the Egyptian Pharaoh Merneptah reads:

O all righteous, come and behold:
Truth has conquered falsehood (with the new king)
The sinners are fallen on their faces . . .
. . . The days are long, the nights have hours,
The months come aright.

As representative of the god of the country, the king is said to fight and defeat the enemies and rule from sea to sea; like the Israelite king, he too is lord of the whole world (which, of course, does not mean that he has the whole world under his rule, but only that he is entitled to it).[2]

Most of these parallels must be explained on the basis of influences from prevalent royal ideologies on the Israelites when they moved from a tribal society, whose affairs were managed by elders and charismatic leaders (judges), to a more institutionalized society governed by kings. Such a transition must have been made under the influence of existing kingdoms, and the Israelite kingdom must to a large extent have been patterned on them. The Old Testament would also lead us to the same conclusion: according to 1 Sam. 8:20, when people ask Samuel to appoint a king over them, they do so in order that they "also may be like other nations." If people wanted a king to be like other nations, then they could hardly have done otherwise than to pattern their kingdom on those that existed around them.

Monotheism and Messianic Hopes

Despite the similarity of the Jewish conception and ideal of kingship with those of the other cultures in the ancient orient, there can be no doubt that this conception and ideal gave rise in a singular way to the global religion, Christianity. There must be something unique in the Jewish tradition that was responsible for the singular development of Jewish messianism. That can be nothing other than a higher, more monotheistic conception of God, which had already become part of the Israelite tradition before the Israelites borrowed from other nations kingship and much that went with it. Despite the fact, attested by the Old Testament, that many Israelites frequently lapsed into idolatry and that the Israelites' conception of God did not rise to pure monotheism[3] until around the 6th century B.C., and never rose completely above nationalism, there is no doubt that by and large they held on to a higher conception of God than the nations round about and they were proud of it. This higher conception of God went with a more earnest and true relation with Him. Responsibilities to and expectations from Him were taken more seriously. In particular, His kingship is taken seriously. As a result, the will of the nation does not disintegrate with the defeats of its earthly kings or even with the collapse of the kingship itself; rather, it hopes for its restoration, for it has faith in the power of its real king. The ideal expectations, previously attached to a reigning king, are not abandoned but are transferred to a near or distant future. The question of why the nation is allowed at all by its all-powerful king, Yahweh, to suffer defeat and other adverse circumstances is answered by the view that these adversities are a punishment for the people's sins. In this way an earnest hope for ideal conditions lived on and grew.

The monolatrous or monotheistic view of Yahweh always occupies a central place in the warnings of future punishment (or reminders of past disasters) and promises of restoration. The punishment comes for many sins (Amos 2:6-15; Hosea 12 etc.) but of these the most frequently mentioned is unfaithfulness to Yahweh, turning to other gods and idols. The restoration comes after turning back to Yahweh and Him alone. From one of the early prophets, Hosea, for example, we read:

When (the tribe of) Ephraim spake trembling, he was exalted in Israel; but when he sinned by worshipping Baal, he died. And now they sin more and more, and have made them molten images of their silver, and idols according to their own understanding . . . Therefore they shall disappear as the morning cloud, and as the early dew that passeth away . . . O Israel, thou hast destroyed thyself; but in me is thine help. I will be thy king: where is any other that may save thee in all thy cities? And thy judges of whom thou sayest, Give me a king and princes? I gave thee kings in mine anger, and took them away in my anger . . . O Israel, return unto Yahweh thy God; for thou hast fallen by thine iniquity . . . Asshur shall not save us, we will not ride upon horses, neither will we say any more to the work of our hands, Ye are our gods: for in thee the fatherless findeth mercy.

I will heal their backsliding, I will love them freely: For mine anger is turned away from them. I will be as the dew unto Israel: he shall grow as the Lily, and cast forth his roots as Lebanon. His branches shall spread, and his beauty shall be as the olive tree, and his smell as Lebanon . . . Ephraim shall say, What have I to do any more with idols. . . .

(Hosea 13:1-11, 14:1-8)

In this passage, the past punishment of the (Jewish) tribe of Ephraim and coming retribution of Israel are connected with worshipping someone other than Yahweh with undivided allegiance and when Ephraim shall say "What have I to do any more with idols?" The same monotheistic and transcendental conception of Yahweh enables the prophet Hosea to see Yahweh as the real king who installs earthly kings or removes them as he wills. For, if it is Yahweh alone who is to be worshipped and who cannot be represented by visible objects, then the earthly king cannot represent Yahweh to the extent that he becomes almost identical with him. This is why, despite the fact that in imitation of other nations the Israelites sometimes referred to their king as a god or a son of god, they never took his divinity as seriously as some other ancient nations like the Egyptians did in the case of their king. This is also why the hopes for ideal conditions could be transferred to an evermore indefinite future and cherished in an earnest way, for hopes attached to such a sublime, jealous, and powerful god, who is above all images and kings and who demands complete devotion and undivided allegiance, cannot be held lightly and easily abandoned.

Messianic Hopes As Restoration Hopes

Messianic expectations arose precisely when these earnestly held hopes for ideal conditions were detached from the reigning king and gradually transferred to an indefinite future. This transference began to happen when the exemplary kingdom established by David and Solomon had disintegrated. It is natural that one of the oldest messianic expectations is the hope that the fallen kingdom of David would some day be restored with all its glory and power. The book of Amos, an early prophet and a contemporary of Hosea, promises:

> In that day I will raise up the tabernacle of David (kingdom of David) which is fallen, and close up the breaches thereof; and I will raise up his ruins and I will build it as in the days of old. That they may possess the remnant of Eden and all the heathen, which are called by my name (i.e. who once called upon my name).
>
> (Amos 9:11-12)

Sometimes the birth of a royal child may evoke hopes that the newly born prince will one day restore the fallen tabernacles of David and establish an everlasting kingdom with justice, peace, and admirable counsel:

> For us a child is born, a son is given; the government shall be upon his shoulder: and his name shall be called Admirable Counselor, Mighty God (or Hero), Everlasting One, Prince of Peace. Of the increase of his government and peace there shall be no end, upon the throne of David, and upon his kingdom, to order it, and to establish it with judgment and with justice from henceforth even for ever.
>
> (Isa. 9:6-7)

Gradually there evolved the idea of the Messiah, the restorer of the Davidic kingdom, as an independent being, as someone who is already there (in heaven) but has yet to be born and perform the work of restoration. This development reached its climax in the post Old Testament period in the apocalyptic works (i.e. Books of Enoch, Ezra, Baruch) where ancient ideas about the figure of Man combine with the Jewish expectation of kingly deliverer to produce a mythological conception of a pre-existent messiah.

Many things that naturally go with a restored Davidic kingdom are specifically predicted. Thus the two existing tribes of Israel, Judah and Ephraim, often in fights with each other, will either merge into each other or live in harmony within a single kingdom (Zech. 9:9-14). Jeremiah promises an unbroken line of priests from the tribe of Levi along with an unbroken line of kings descending from David (33:17-18). And, of course, there is the promise that Israel will be materially prosperous and politically strong and independent kingdom that will conquer or dominate all or some of the other nations either as a result of war or through the nations' voluntary recognition of Israel's superiority.

In its promise of restoration, the Israelite religion had reached a point of no return. No matter what disintegration the nation suffered, it could not let go of this hope. If their seditious and rebellious actions against the dominating super-powers of the time resulted in their exile or the destruction of such basic institutions as the Jerusalem temple, this did not lead to the abandonment of the national hopes, but only resulted in a more tenacious adherence to them. The post-exilic prophets could easily promise that the exiles would return and the temple would be rebuilt.

Tendency Towards Universalism

With time the messianic hopes ceased to be merely hopes for restoration, for a return to the good old days when Israelites prospered as a kingdom under a great and righteous king David. They began to acquire new elements and the prophets' imagination was able to create possibilities for the future radically different from any realized in the past. Ezekiel could talk of a new heart (36:26) and Jeremiah of a new covenant (31:31-34). Some prophets showed a tendency towards universalism and saw other nations taking part in the future salvation. Related with this is the doctrine of a Remnant according to which only a righteous section of the people of Israel will be saved, while the rest will perish. If the better elements in other nations could share salvation with Israel, then the worst of the Israelites could perish with their counterparts among the Gentiles.

This tendency towards universalism was made possible by the tendency toward monotheism. For if there is only one true God whose power extends over all peoples and all creation, then the divisions among various nations or races maintained by the worship of different deities must in principle cease to be absolute and it should be possible to think of the people of God as a community not once and for all identified with a particular race or nation, but as one from which members of any group can be excluded and into which members of any group can be included, depending on their moral behavior or spiritual condition. It is not chance that when Jewish monotheism reaches its climax, so does the universalism of Jewish messianism. Nowhere in the Old Testament do we find universalism reaching the heights that it does in the following passage from Second Isaiah, the prophet who is the first Israelite on record to give a clear expression of the monotheist's position:

> And He (God) said (to the prophet): It is a light thing that thou shouldest be my servant to raise up the tribes of Jacob, and to restore the preserved of Israel: I will also give thee for a light to the Gentiles that thou mayest be my salvation unto the end of the earth.
>
> (Isa. 49:6)

Monotheism and universal salvation are mentioned together in the following passage from Second Isaiah:

> They have no knowledge that set up the wood of their graven images, and pray unto a god that cannot save. . . . who hath declared this from ancient time? Who hath told it from that time? Am not I the Lord? And there is no God else beside me; a just God and a Saviour; there is none beside me. Look unto me, and be ye saved, all the ends of the earth: *for I am God, and there is none else.*
>
> (Isa. 45:20-22)

But even at its height, the Old Testament monotheism is not true monotheism and its universalism not true universalism. For, even in Second Isaiah, it is Yahweh, the god worshipped by Israel, who becomes the only and universal God and drives other gods out of existence. Consequently, Israel retains its unique and superior position among the nations of the world and Second Isaiah can say:

(Kings and queens of other nations) shall bow down to thee with their face to the earth, and lick the dust of thy feet (O Israel).

(Isa. 49:23)

For that nation and kingdom that will not serve thee shall perish yea, these nations shall be utterly wasted.

(Isa. 60:12)

In this passage we may justifiably take "serve thee" to mean "worship thee O nation of Israel" for the Old Testament does give a strong impression of the nation of Israel as a kind of idol. Thus despite the profession of monotheism in some parts of the Old Testament, there are in actuality two gods in the Jewish holy book: God and the People of Israel. On the basis of the Old Testament one could formulate, with more justification, a doctrine of God's duality i.e. one in two and two in one, than one can formulate the doctrine of the Trinity of God on the basis of the New Testament.

Corresponding to these two gods of the Old Testament are the two types of messianic hopes that, like the gods themselves, are inseparably confused with each other, namely, the nationalistic hopes and the universalist hopes. These two types of messianic hopes in turn correspond to two separate developments in subsequent history, namely, the development started in Christianity and consummated in Islam and the struggle of the Jews to survive as a people and realize their ancient national dreams, which has in our times led to the formation of the State of Israel. In later chapters (IV - VI) we shall discuss in some detail the two types of messianic hopes and the developments they inspired in subsequent history.

NOTES

1. Especially by S. Mowinckel, *He That Cometh*, (trans. G. W. Anderson Oxford, 1956); A. Bentzen, *King and Messiah* (Lutterworth Press, London, 1955); Joseph Klausner, *The Messianic Idea in Israel*, trans. W. F. Stinespring (London, 1956; and C. A. Briggs, *Messianic Prophecy* (Edinburgh, 1886).

2. For a detailed study of kingship concepts in the ancient Orient, see I. Engnell, *Studies in Divine Kingship* (Uppsala, 1943); H. Frankfort, *Kingship and the Gods* (Chicago, 1948). Our summary is based on the one in Helmer Ringgren, *The Messiah in the Old Testament* (SCM Press, London, 1956), pp. 20-23.

3. The doctrine that there is one and only one God does not find its full and conscious expression in the Old Testament until Second Isaiah, the part of the Book of Isaiah (Chapters 40-66) written about two hundred years after the time of (the first) Isaiah (8th century B.C.) by an anonymous prophet. The Old Testament has preserved traditions from the times when the Israelites did not conceive of God in monotheistic, transcendent terms. The Book of Genesis does not hesitate to report that the Patriarchs like Jacob had in their houses figurines of clay representing gods (31:30-35). Even after Moses, Yahweh could be conceived as a god of a particular people with his sovereignty limited to a particular land. The command: "Thou shalt have no other god before me" (Deut. 5:7) was long understood by most Israelites to mean that Yahweh would not tolerate any rivals on his own territory and would not accept divided allegiance from his people or worshippers. In other lands and for other people the sovereignty of other gods could be recognized. When David is driven out of "Yahweh's land" he feels that he is forced to serve gods of other lands; he also asks Saul not to let him be killed on foreign soil, "away from Yahweh" (1 Sam. 26:19-20).

It was only gradually proclaimed that the supremacy of Yahweh extended over the whole world of men and things and that his hand was active in the affairs of all nations whether they knew it or not. Amos may be the first to give expression to this idea when he says that the same God who brought Israel out of Egypt also brought the Philistines from Caphtor and the Syrians from Kir (9:7). A little later, First Isaiah sees the hand of Yahweh in the westward advance of the hosts of Assyria (5:26). For Jeremiah, the vast empire of Nebuchadnezzar is Yahweh's gift (27:5-11) and for Second Isaiah, the rise of the Persian Emperor Cyrus is a work of Yahweh and the Emperor is called Yahweh's shepherd or anointed (Isa. 44:24-45:25). Nature, like men, also came gradually under the absolute sovereignty of Yahweh. The prophet Hosea declares that it is Yahweh and none other who gives the corn and wine and oil (2:9).

And as the sovereignty of Yahweh progressively expanded beyond the boundaries of the land of the Israelites, the gods of other lands and peoples were progressively degraded until they were not just deities irrelevant to the Israelites or rivals of Yahweh but non-entities. Then Second Isaiah could express the monotheistic idea of God by saying as a mouthpiece of Yahweh: "I am the first and I am the last: and besides me there is no god" (Isa. 44:6). But this development is not a linear one in which older less sublime ideas are completely eliminated from tradition once a higher idea finds expression: rather, throughout the Old Testament we find older ideas surviving along with more developed concepts.

Chapter II

The Meaning of Messianic Prophecies

Christian Use of Messianic Prophecies

T raditional Christian interpretation, still held officially by many Churches and shared by many of their members, sees most of the messianic prophecies as literal words of God giving exact details of future events. The trend for this interpretation was set firmly by the New Testament itself which builds up the belief in the Messiahship of Jesus by showing how various messianic predictions in the Old Testament were fulfilled by events in the life and work of Jesus. So enthusiastic are some New Testament writers to fulfill in Jesus' life that which "is written" that if a word in a Scriptural sentence reminds them of Jesus they can ignore its intended meaning and modify history drastically to "fulfill" it in some way. For example, just because of a reference to "my (Yahweh's) son" which is often used of Israel in the Old Testament, Matthew sees in Hosea's words: "Out of Egypt have I called my son," a prophecy about Jesus and, without any basis in historical fact, makes Joseph and Mary take baby Jesus to Egypt and then return to Palestine after Herod's death (2:14-15), while the fact is that Hosea was referring simply to the well-known exodus of the Israelites from Egypt.

There are many such uses of "messianic prophecies" in the Gospels. They might, in earlier times, have helped increase faith in Jesus, but for the modern readers of the Gospels they are generally an embarrassment[1] and serve only to point out the error of reading Scriptural passages as if they were written with some future person's life and work in mind.

Even where there are exact correspondences between some predictions and certain historical events connected with Jesus, one cannot draw any meaningful conclusions from them. For one thing, such correspondences can also be found for other semitic religious figures such as Prophet Muhammad (see Chapters IV - VI and Appendix I). For another, points of agreement between predictions and historical events lose their significance when one also notes, as one must, the points of disagreement that are often found in the same book and even in the same prediction. For example, the Song of the suffering servant of the Lord (Is. 52:13-53:12; see Appendix I) has been applied by Christians as a prediction of Jesus' vicarious suffering, but a number of details in the song and other predictions by the same prophet stand in glaring contradiction to the historical events connected with Jesus and his church. Thus the song predicts that the suffering servant will escape death and live to see his descendents and be a mighty man, dividing spoils with the strong (Is. 53:10-12), whereas according to Christian tradition, Jesus died celibate without leaving any descendents or dividing spoils with mighty men. Some chapters later, the same prophet makes a prediction about pork eaters which would exclude almost all Christians from salvation (Is. 66:17). When such details are noticed, the reference to the vicarious suffering of the servant of the Lord ceases to have any far-reaching significance for the Christian belief about Jesus' suffering, other than that the idea of vicarious suffering was not an original contribution of Christianity but was known and acceptable to Jews in some pre-Christian times also.

Unreliability of Messianic Prophecies As Predictions

The failure of Christianity to show convincingly that Jesus and his work fulfilled exactly and literally the Old Testament messianic predictions is quite understandable because most of these predictions were either never meant to be fulfilled in that way, or were not inspired by a genuine knowledge of the future. The Old Testament contains many predictions proven to be false. For Example, according to 2 Sam. 7:13-15, God promised David that his kingdom would last for ever. In reality, nothing like a Jewish kingdom with a king of David's line has existed in the last two and a half thousand years and it is now even difficult to point to any authentic descendent of David.

In the time of King Nebuchadnezzar, prophet Jeremiah predicted that the Babylonian king would invade Egypt and burn Egypt's gods or carry them away (Jer. 43:8-13). The prediction was never fulfilled.

Haggai promises Zerubbabel, the governor of Judah in the later decades of the sixth century B.C., that God will shake the heavens and the earth" and overthrow kingdoms and end their power," and instead install Zerubbabel as the ruler of the world (Haggai 2:21-23). In reality Zerubbabel disappeared from the stage of history as no more than a governor of tiny Judah, whose rule depended on the patronage of the Persian king, Darius.

In addition to the messianic prophecies proven to be false, the Old Testament is also full of obvious contradictions in its picture of the messianic future. We shall encounter many examples of this as our study proceeds, but here we may mention only one case: According to Ezekiel's vision of the messianic future (44:6-9), no foreigner will be allowed to enter the Jerusalem sanctuary, while Micah 4:2 foresees many foreign people coming to the temple and taking part in the worship of Yahweh.

The presence of numerous false and contradictory prophecies in the Old Testament warns us that we cannot expect all its messianic prophecies to come true.

Another thing to be kept in mind while reading the Old Testament prophecies is that not all of them are to be interpreted literally. This is true not only of dreams of the future such as we find in the Book of Daniel (7) but also of some other forms of prediction. For example, when the Book of Isaiah (18:7) promises that foreigners from distant lands will bring burnt offerings to Jerusalem, it is legitimate to interpret this to mean that foreigners will join the Jews in the worship of the One God and will come to Jerusalem for that worship without expecting it to take place in the same ritual form in which it took place in the time of Isaiah, or to be accompanied by ritual offerings. For one thing, Isaiah himself says that making burnt offerings is not the essential thing (1:14-20). For another, we cannot expect a prophet, even when he is inspired by a genuine knowledge of the future, to see that future except in terms of reference to the present, which may or may not be adequate for the description of future events. As Briggs[2] notes, "The prophet cannot emancipate himself from his human nature and surroundings. He cannot divest himself of his historic position and circumstances . . . Hence his prediction clothes itself with the local, the temporal, and the circumstantial dress. The future events cannot be presented in prediction in the circumstances of the future and from the point of view of the future. If that were so, it would no longer be prediction, but history." The distinction between history and prediction should prevent us from seeking an exact and literal fulfillment even if we can assume actual knowledge of the future on the part of the prophet.

But while prophets can at times foresee future events, especially those near at hand,[3] it is impossible to isolate from the mass of messianic predictions those that were inspired by an actual knowledge of the future. In any case, such genuine predictions must be very, very few, considering the numerous contradictions in detail that are found in the various messianic passages, and considering the fact that a careful study of the history of messianic tradition reveals that it was never really a concern of the prophets to foretell the future. "Their business," as noted by Kuenen, "is not to communicate what shall happen, but to insist upon what ought to happen. The maintenance of the Yahweh worship as they comprehended it - that is what they had in view in the whole course of their activity."[4]

More specifically, the concern of the prophets is to maintain worship of, and obedience to, Yahweh as the transcendent and only God of the Israelites by assuring them that Yahweh's obedient worshippers will prosper, while those who are disobedient to him or worship other gods will be punished. In other words, the prophets are primarily concerned with revealing certain conceptions of God, His worship and moral demands, and of the accountability of man. The key to the correct interpretation of messianic prophecy is to make these conceptions the primary object of our attention and not the events predicted. The predictions enter into the picture largely because the style of expression of traditional and popular religion required a concrete expression of the way Yahweh would redeem his true worshippers and punish others: the prophets could not just state the principle of redemption and punishment in general terms, but had to appeal to the imagination of their readers with concrete promises to the righteous and, similarly, concrete warnings to the sinners and idolaters.

The concrete promises and warnings were inspired least of all by actual knowledge of the future. They are rather to be explained in terms of the following factors:

1) The prophet's conception of God and His moral demands. For example, if a prophet viewed his god as a national god existing along with the gods of other nations, he could view the future salvation as a state of peace among various peoples, each walking in the name of its own god (Micah 4:5), while if he viewed God in universal terms he could foresee a time when "every knee will bow before him and every tongue shall swear to him" (Isa. 45:23).

2) The historical circumstances in which the prophet lived. Biblical historians have shown how, like everything else, messianic prophecies are generally tied to the historical situation in which they were written. Messianic prophecies become more or less political, spiritual, nationalistic, or universalistic according to the socio-political conditions. Prophets like Amos, Hosea, etc., who lived when there existed some kind of Israelite kingdom, concerned themselves with the spiritual and moral

condition of the nation. But of prophets like Ezekiel and Second Isaiah, who prophesied, for the most part, after the Babylonians had destroyed Israel's institutions and exiled her king, the main concern was survival of the nation. Moral reform or repentance could be postponed until after the threat to the existence of the nation had passed (Ezek. 16:60-62). For earlier prophets repentance was a condition of the redemption of the nation but both Ezekiel and Second Isaiah promised redemption without any such condition, as if Yahweh was *obligated* to redeem Israel for reasons of his own, "for his name's sake" (Ezek. 36:20-21; 11:17-18; Isa. 48:9,11). Again, Ezekiel saw the Gentiles bringing only destruction on Israel and so he has a very nationalistic attitude, cold to foreigners, while Second Isaiah prophesied in the time of the Persian king Cyrus who let the Israelites return to their land and treated them very favorably, and so he shows a thawed attitude towards Gentiles and has a very universalist outlook.

3) The third factor that determines the messianic predictions of a prophet is the past tradition, i.e. the predictions he received from earlier prophets. These provided the material which the prophet, by the use of his own inspired imagination, moulded and enlarged to serve his purpose.

The Meaning of Fulfillment

Since the central elements in the messianic prophecy are the religious conceptions of God, His moral demands, and His justice, the predictions that give a concrete expression to these conceptions are not reliable as descriptions of the future. The fulfillment of the messianic prophecy in subsequent religious history should not be thought of as the actual happening of the events predicted, but as the completion, perfection, and victory of the religious principles enshrined in it. The religious principles contained in the messianic prophecy did need completion, perfection, and victory.

The Old Testament does not carry, for example, the conception of God to its highest possible level and, moreover, contains older, less sublime, national conceptions along with more developed universal ideas. The same can be said of God's moral demands and the manifestation of His justice, which are not conceived in the Old Testament in sufficiently individualistic terms: God's moral demands, His judgement, and salvation are largely understood to be for nations as a whole and not for persons individually. In these and other directions, the Old Testament left the need for its religious principles to be further developed. There was also a need for a purer and more universal expression of religious principles, an expression free from older imperfect ideas and relatively free from the context of the peculiar history of a single nation, in order that the whole of mankind could receive those principles and benefit from them. These needs were fulfilled, as I hope to make clear in later chapters, through Islam, with Christianity playing a preparatory and helping role.

It is not just the religious principles enshrined in the messianic predictions that needed to be perfected, but also the predictions themselves. For religious principles are often inseparable from the predictions they give rise to, and cannot evolve to a higher stage without the predictions themselves undergoing a change. Thus in Micah 4:5, a passage we have already cited in another context, the time of salvation is viewed as a time of peace among nations, all walking in the names of their gods. This prediction itself must undergo modification if the underlying nationalistic and polytheistic conception of deity is to give way to a more developed conception. It is, therefore, no mere chance that writers who had a monotheistic conception of God hoped, in contrast to Micah 4:5, for a time when all nations would join together in the worship of the one God and live peacefully (Is. 19:18-25, 45:23). As another example, the Old Testament views the messianic future in political terms as victory and prosperity in this world for the righteous worshippers of Yahweh and a defeat and destruction for others. This is because God's moral demands and justice are generally viewed on a national basis, that is, nations as a whole are judged in history according to how they *as nations* respond to God's moral demands. But when in some circles in post Old Testament time, religion is more individualized, with each individual considered responsible for his own moral conduct, the political this-worldly view of the messianic future had to give way to a suprahistorical, other-worldly view of the time of judgment and salvation, such as is implied in the belief in resurrection, paradise, and hell; for only through such a view of the age to come could the principle be expressed that each and every individual must bear the consequences of his moral conduct.

One result of the above observation that messianic prophecies are a part of a progressing history of revelation, in which both the pictures of the future and the religious ideas presupposed in them undergo changes, is that in the light of the development in man's religious thought after the Old Testament was completed, we have the right to judge the continued validity and relevance of various messianic prophecies. For in a progressing history of ideas of any kind, we must expect some ideas to become obsolete, especially if we encounter contradictions as we do in the case of the Old Testament prophecies. Passing judgement on sections of the Old Testament as to their continued validity or relevance has, in fact, been found unavoidable even by Jews and Christians who give the whole of the Jewish scripture the authority of the word of God. Thus, ever since Paul became victorious over his rivals, the Christians have decided that many of the Old Testament laws such as those governing food, sabbath, circumcision, etc., no longer have any validity and most of the Jews, too, will find some of these laws to have no relevance today.

When we judge the messianic prophecies in a similar spirit we find certain sections of them as obsolete as some of the Old Testament rules and regulations. For example, it is expected in the Old Testament (Amos 9:11-12; Isa. 9:6-7; Micah 5:2; Jer. 33:17-18 etc.) that one day the whole world will be subjugated by the Jews, who will all be gathered in the land their ancestors inhabited centuries ago and will be ruled by a descendent of David, and that this king of David's line will necessarily be born in Bethlehem, the city of David, and will establish an everlasting dynasty. We are dealing here with hopes of national glory and power, which we cannot today find meaningful in any way. Such hopes offend the universalist way of viewing man and God that Islam and the best of the teachings of Christianity and Judaism have given to the world.

One may also wonder whether there was ever any worthwhile religious value in such prophecies - why should it ever matter, for example, where the restorer of David's kingdom should be born? And if this is not reason enough for regarding these expectations as irrelevant, in this age at least, then surely it must be enough to add that they have no chance of coming true. For today there are no authentic descendents of David out of whom the restorer of this kingdom could arise; moreover, most of the Jews have always found it impossible to leave their countries and gather together in Palestine, not to talk of the insurmountable difficulties for any one nation to acquire ruling power over the whole world and maintain it forever.

In contrast to the purely nationalistic hopes for the Israelites' political supremacy over the world, there are some prophecies in the Old Testament that contain nobler expectations and higher conceptions of God and man. Although never completely rising above nationalism, they hope for universal peace and prosperity and foresee a time when nations will join together in the worship of the one transcendent God. It is these universalist hopes that were destined to form the basis of the best developments in the subsequent history of religion. The conceptions of God and man and man's future contained in them were successively carried to full development through Christianity and Islam. They are ultimately responsible for much of the constructive talk today about international peace and happiness. Even as predictions they have found impressive fulfillment in the developments inspired in history by Islam. In chapters IV and V we shall elaborate these points, from which we can conclude that only those messianic prophecies that contain sufficiently sublime religious conceptions have found fulfillment and continued relevance. Messianic foresight, in the last analysis, was religious insight.

NOTES

1. This is true even of such reverend readers of the Bible as C. H. Dodd (see his *The Authority of the Bible* (Fontana Books, 1960), p. 195.

2. C. A. Briggs, *The Messianic Prophecy* (Edinburgh, 1886), p. 57.

3. This is shown most convincingly by the following prediction in the Qur'an: "The Roman Empire has been defeated in a nearby land. But they after this defeat will be victorious - within a few (less than ten) years. With God is the decision, in the past and in the future . . ." (30:2-4).

   The prediction relates to the war between Roman and Persian Empires (610-628 A.C.), in which Christian Rome at first suffered heavy defeats, losing Aleppo, Antioch, and the chief Syrian cities, including Damascus, in 611 A.C., Jerusalem in 614-15 and Egypt in 616. By the year 622 the Persian armies had reached Tripoli in North Africa, ravaged Asia Minor and were standing at the gates of Constantinople. Then the Roman emperor Heraclius conceived a series of brilliant moves that enabled him to win some decisive victories.

   The Roman defeat in a land near Arabia mentioned in the Quranic passage cited above is the loss of Jerusalem in 614-5 A.C., shortly before the passage was revealed. After conquering Jerusalem, the Persians, assisted by the Jewish inhabitants, pillaged the city, burnt its churches, massacred Christians, and insulted their holy places and relics. This greatly pleased the Meccan enemies of Islam and increased their own persecution of Muslims, who favored Christianity far above the Meccan or Persian religion. The Qur'an revealed that the Persian victories were temporary and that within a few years the tables would be turned. In 622 A.C. Heraclius routed the surprised Persians at Issus and in 623-625 he was campaigning right in the heart of Persia.

4. Kuenen, *Prophets and Prophecy in Israel* (London, 1871), p. 344. Even scholars who see some validity in messianic prophecies as predictions of the future recognize that the concern of the messianic prophecies is primarily religious. Thus Tholuck remarks that "it is not prediction of the accidental, but of that which is of religious necessity, which is the essential thing in Hebrew prophecy" (quoted from C. A. Briggs, op.cit., p. 44).

Chapter III

The Messianic Trinity
of John, Jesus, and Muhammad

T he universalist messianic prophecies in the Old Testament find
fulfillment through the Islamic revelation brought by the Prophet
Muhammad (SAWS) with the work of John the Baptist and Jesus
Christ (AS), i.e. Christianity, playing a preparatory and helping role. This
is a claim that we shall consider in subsequent chapters in the light of
the Old Testament prophecies themselves, but in the present chapter
we show that this claim has the authority of Jesus Christ (AS) and the
Prophet Muhammad (SAWS).

Jesus taught, as we shall see, that the fulfillment of messianic prophecies began with the appearance of John the Baptist, continued in his
own work, and would be consummated with the universal manifestation of the perfect Man (or the Son of man, as the Gospels too literally
translated the original Aramaic title Barnasha). The same view can be
held on the basis of the Qur'an, which teaches furthermore that the
universal manifestation of the Perfect Man expected by Jesus and others
before him took place with the advent of the Prophet Muhammad
(SAWS). The three religious figures thus form a kind of "messianic trinity"
through which the hopes of earlier generations of men are being fulfilled. The idea of a trinity of messianic figures is also found in some
pre-Christian Jewish traditions. We shall now present evidence for these
conclusions.

John The Baptist As a Messianic Figure
in the Teachings of Jesus and Muhammad

For the authentic teaching of Jesus (AS) our primary sources are the
Gospel of Mark and a compilation of sayings generally designated by the
letter Q (from the German 'Quelle' for 'source').[1] Both of these sources
contain sayings that consider the coming of John the Baptist to be in
fulfillment of the messianic predictions. Thus, using a Q saying, Matthew
and Luke say:

From the days of John the Baptist until now the kingdom of heaven is forced and men of force seize it. For all the prophets and the law prophesied until John.

(Matthew 11:12-13)

The law and the prophets were until John; since then the kingdom of God is preached and everyone is forcing his way into it.

(Luke 16:16)

The original form of the saying behind these two versions is extremely hard to determine, but it seems clear that the original saying regarded the coming of John the Baptist as marking a decisive point in time, closing the age of prophecy and ushering in the age of fulfillment. Consistent with this, the Gospel of Mark identifies the Baptist with Elijah who, according to long held Jewish expectations, was to return as a messianic figure to herald the age of fulfillment. Replying to the disciples' question, "Why do the scribes say that Elijah must first come?," Jesus says in Mark 9:12-13, "Elijah indeed, coming first, will restore all things . . . But I say unto you, that Elijah is indeed come (in the person of John the Baptist) . . ."

These and other similar sayings in Mark and Q have been analysed in some detail in my *Jesus and the Messianic Figures*, but here we may remark that the combined attestation by our two primary sources alone enables us to attribute to Jesus with considerable probability the view that John the Baptist came in fulfillment of the messianic prophecy.

The same view can be attributed to the Qur'an with even greater confidence. The Qur'an says (3:39) that the Prophet Yahya (John) came verifying "a word from Allah," which can be interpreted only in one of the following two ways, each of which implies that he came as a messianic figure:

(a) "a word from Allah" means a promise of Allah (cf. 10:64), that is, an earlier prophecy; in this case the meaning is that the Prophet Yahya came fulfilling earlier expectations, in other words, as a messianic figure;

(b) in 3:45 Jesus is called "a word from Allah," and so Yahya's verifying "a word from Allah" may mean that he came bearing witness to Jesus (AS), a reference to the Christian tradition that Jesus was the Messiah and John was his Elijah-type forerunner, which again makes him a kind of messianic figure.

Jesus As a Messianic Figure in His Own Teachings and in the Qur'an

It is not certain what Jesus thought of his own messianic role, but one thing is certain. He did not come forward as the final and only saviour, though he later became that in Church doctrine. At the same time, the very fact that Jesus was active when, according to his own view, the age of fulfillment of the messianic prophecies had been ushered in by John, would suggest that he thought of his work too as partly fulfilling these prophecies. This is supported by specific sayings considered to be authentic by almost every New Testament scholar:

> Blessed are the eyes which see the things that ye see: For I tell you, that many prophets and kings have desired to see these things which ye see, and have not seen them ...
> (Q: Matt. 13:16-17; Luke 10:23-24)

> But if by the finger of God I cast out devils, then the kingdom of God has come upon you (i.e. is standing at the door).
> (Q: Matt. 12:28; Luke 11:20)

> The blind receive their sight, and the lame walk, and lepers are cleansed, and the deaf hear, and dead are raised up, and the poor have the gospel (message of salvation) preached to them.
> (Q: Matt. 11:5; Luke 7:22)

In these passages Jesus is alluding to such Jewish messianic expectations as the defeat of Satan and elimination of disease and of joy among the poor[2] and is suggesting at the same time that these expectations are finding fulfillment through his highly successful exorcisms and miraculous healing of the sick and his preaching of a message of salvation to the poor and the meek (Matt. 5:1-12). Jesus does not assume here any messianic role that can be defined clearly in terms of the earlier tradition, although there are some other passages in our two primary sources (Mark 9:33-39; 10:35-27; 11:1-11) and Q (Luke 22:28-30) which, if historical and authentic, would allow us to go further and attribute to Jesus the assumption of the definite identity of the national Messiah, the Davidic "king of the Jews" (Mark 15:26) who was to come and restore the Jewish kingdom. But whether or not one goes as far as attributing to Jesus such a definite view of his messianic role, the sayings quoted above and the whole character of our main sources and of the Christian proclamation from its very beginning provide sufficient basis to hold that Jesus regarded himself as one of the agents of the fulfillment of messianic prophecies.

The teachings of Prophet Muhammad (SAWS) are in agreement. The Qur'an accepts "the Messiah" as a name or a title of Jesus (3:45; 5:78 etc.). It does not define the sense of the title "the Messiah" nor does it tell the story of Jesus in a way that would allow us to recognize Jesus as the Messiah in any established sense of the title. Nevertheless, we would be completely justified in concluding from the Qur'anic application of the title "the Messiah" to Jesus that Jesus is a messianic figure.

The Prophet Muhammad As a Promised Figure

We now consider the basis in the teachings of Jesus (AS) and the Qur'an for the view that Prophet Muhammad (SAWS) was the last of the three agents of Allah (SAWS) whom He raised to fulfill the hopes contained in the Old Testament messianic prophecy.

As far as Jesus' teachings are concerned, it must be recognized that we cannot expect him to talk about the Prophet as if he could clearly visualize that particular individual six centuries before his arrival on the stage of history. Such is not the nature of Judeo-Christian messianic prophecy. That prophecy is inspired by certain hopes expressed in concrete pictures of the future, pictures that are often drawn from past traditions rather than from a knowledge of the future (see Chap. II for a more detailed discussion of the nature and meaning of the messianic prophecy).. The way in which Jesus' sayings do provide a basis for regarding Prophet Muhammad (SAWS) as a messianic figure is that they clearly indicate that Jesus (AS) did not think of his own mission as either final or universal, but rather looked forward to a final and universal saviour as someone other than himself.

Gospel criticism has established conclusively that Jesus (AS) did not think of his mission in universal terms and left this world with his attention totally restricted to the Jewish people. There is no tradition in Q and no authentic saying in Mark which suggests that Jesus (AS) addressed or directed his mission in some other way to the whole of mankind. But we do know of a bitter dispute in the early Church concerning whether there should be a Christian mission to nations other than the Jews, a dispute that would never have occurred had Jesus started a universal mission. The saying in Matthew which prohibits the disciples from preaching among the Gentiles because Jesus was sent only to "the lost sheep of the house of Israel" (10:5-6) is a product of this dispute; it was invented by Jews who did not want a Gentile mission. In opposition, the proponents of the Gentile mission produced the story in Mark (7:24-30) about a sick Gentile girl whom Jesus first refused to heal because she was not Jewish but later agreed to heal. In this story healing represents the Christian mission; Jesus' refusal to heal a Gentile girl relates to the fact that there was no question of a Christian mission to non-Jews during the life of Jesus, and his willingness later to perform the healing reflects the Church's claim that after his death when he became the Risen Lord, Jesus gave her authority for such a mission.

It is consistent with Jesus' limited view of his own mission that he expected a more universal messianic figure to come after him. It is now recognized by many of the most reputed New Testament scholars such as Rudolf Bultmann,[3] John Knox,[4] F. Hahn,[5] H. E. Todt,[6] A. J. B. Higgins,[7] and R. H. Fuller[8] that Jesus did not identify himself with the figure of Man or the Son of Man (Barnasha or Geber) mentioned so frequently in the Gospels, but rather looked forward to this person as a future figure other than himself. This is shown by the following Q saying, a version of which is also quoted independently by Mark (8:38):

Whosoever therefore acknowledges me before men, him shall the Man (Barnasha) also acknowledge before the angels of God. But he who denies me before men will be denied before the angels of God.

(Luke 12:8-9; cf. Matt 10:32-33)

This distinction that Jesus makes between himself and Man (Barnasha) and between his mission now and Man's mission in the future is crystal clear. We are dealing here with an authentic saying. Apart from the fact that it has the combined support of our two primary sources, the authenticity of the saying is assured by the argument that the Church, which liked to heap on Jesus all kinds of messianic titles and functions, could never have invented a saying talking about a future messianic figure other than himself.

It is also extremely significant that the Essenes, a Jewish sect that flourished before and during the time of Jesus, knew of Man and applied to him titles borrowed from Isaiah 9:6, including the title Pele Yoetz (Admirable or Marvellous Counsellor). The significance of this lies in the fact that the figure promised in John 14:15-17, 14:25-26, 15:26-27, 16:7-15 as a future figure other than Jesus bears the title Parakletos, which is a possible Greek equivalent of Counsellor and that this figure has many other similarities to the Essenes' Man.[9] From this we can conclude that the Parakletos was originally not the Holy Spirit, as secondary interpretations make him in John, but identical with the messianic figure of Man. This provides independent evidence that Jesus looked forward to the

coming of Man after him. The most probable form of the authentic tradition behind John's passages about the Parakletos is:[10]

> I have yet many things to say unto you, but ye cannot bear them
> now. Howbeit when (the Counsellor), the Spirit of truth, is come,
> he will guide you into all truth; for he shall not speak of himself,
> but whatsoever he shall hear, that shall he speak; and he will show
> you things to come. [The "Spirit of truth" was another title of
> Man.]
>
> (John 16:12-13)

The title Pele or Admirable used by the Essenes for Man on the basis
of Isaiah 9:6 also entered Christian expectation of Man, probably through
Jesus' own usage. The following verse from the Qur'an also testifies to
this:

> Behold! Jesus son of Mary said: O Children of Israel! I am the mes-
> senger of God (sent) to you; (I have come) confirming that which
> (I find) before me of the Torah and giving the good news of another
> messenger to come after me, his name being Admirable (Ahmad)
> (61:6).

For Jesus, Man was the final and universal figure. He does not speak
of any figure after Man and says, according to an authentic saying in
Q (Matt. 24:26-28; Luke 17:23-24) that the coming of Man will be a global
event to be observed in the east and the west like lightning in heaven.

We now turn to the Islamic basis for viewing Prophet Muhammad
(SAWS) as a figure who fulfills earlier expectations, that is, as a promised
or messianic figure. Without using any Old Testament messianic terms,
the Qur'an makes it perfectly clear that the Prophet's coming fulfills
expectations of all earlier religions. We have already quoted Qur'an 61:6
where it is implied that the Prophet (SAWS) was the messenger Admirable who was promised by Jesus (AS) and who was expected by some
Christians even in the time of the Prophet. In the following verse Allah
says that the Prophet (SAWS) fulfilled the (messianic) hopes in both the
Jewish and Christian scriptures:

> With My punishment I visit whom I will, but My mercy extends
> to all things. That (mercy) I shall ordain for those (among the peo-
> ple of the Book) who ... follow the Messenger, the unlettered
> Prophet, whom they find mentioned in (their own tradition) in the
> Torah and the Gospel ...
>
> (7:157)

The Qur'an teaches that the following prayer made by Abraham and Ishmael after building the House of Allah in Mecca was fulfilled with the coming of Muhammad (SAWS):

> Our Lord! Send amongst them (our descendents, the Arabs) an Apostle from among them who will rehearse Thy signs to them and instruct them in Scripture and Wisdom and sanctify them. For Thou indeed art the Mighty and the Wise (2:129).

Finally, the following verses state that all earlier prophets, their followers, and other peoples with religious knowledge were aware of a "promise of Allah" that was fulfilled with the revelation brought by the Prophet Muhammad (SAWS):

> Say, Whether ye believe in it (i.e. the Qur'an) or not, it is a fact that those who possessed knowledge before it fall on their faces in humble prostration when it is recited to them. And they say, Glory to our Lord! Truly has the promise of our Lord been fulfilled! (17:107-108)

> Behold! Allah took the covenant of the prophets (saying), I give you a book and Wisdom. Then comes to you an Apostle who will confirm what is with you (of the true religion); do believe in him and help him. Allah said, "Do you agree and take this covenant of Mine binding on you?" They said, "We agree." He said, "Then bear witness, and I am also a witness along with you."
>
> (3:81)

This last highly mystical verse looks at the whole history of revelation in a single glance. The message is that one of the functions of all the numerous prophets sent in various lands and among various peoples was to prepare the way for the advent of the last and universal prophet. They contributed to this preparation in two ways: firstly, their teaching contained something of the divine knowledge and wisdom and provided the context for the final, complete, and perfect expression of the religious truth, and, secondly, they generated or confirmed the hopes for the advent of such a final, complete, and perfect revelation.

In addition, to the Qur'an, the Prophetic Hadith also contain many traditions where the coming of the Prophet (SAWS) is related to earlier expectations. We quote here one such tradition, on the basis of which we can make an identification between the Prophet Muhammad (SAWS) and the figure of Man expected not only in Jewish and Christian tradition, but also in other ancient religions:

I shall be the first to come forth when men are raised to life (at the Day of Judgement); I shall be their leader when they come before Allah and their advocate in their speechlessness; I shall be the one asked to intercede for them when they are restrained and the one who gives glad tidings when they despair; honor and keys will on that day be in my hands.

(Mishkat Al-Masabih, Book 24, Chap. 18, Section 2)

All the characteristics of the Prophet (SAWS) mentioned in this tradition are expected of Man in the pre-Islamic religions. Thus Man is often conceived in Iranian religion as the first of God's creation who will also be the first to rise on the day of resurrection.[11] The role of intercession on the Day of Judgement is expected of Man in the saying of Jesus (Luke 12:8-9, quoted earlier) in which Man is expected to acknowledge (i.e. recommend for salvation) some men before God and His angels. That the "honor and keys" on the Day of Judgement will be in the hands of the Prophet (SAWS) recalls the vision of Daniel in which Man is presented before God and "given authority, honor, and royal power" (Dan. 7:13-14).

The Expectation of a Messianic Trinity in the Jewish Tradition

From the above we can conclude that the teachings of Jesus (AS) and Muhammad (SAWS) provide the basis for speaking of three messianic figures and for identifying these figures with John, Jesus, and Muhammad (AS). Other religions also knew of a trinity of messianic figures. Joseph Klausner[12] says that the Persian tradition knows of the threefold Sayoshyant (a Persian equivalent of the Man and the Messiah) or three Sayoshyants. The Jewish tradition also contains expectations of three messianic figures: a priest like Elijah or Aaron, a king like David, and prophet like Moses. Thus in the Dead Sea Scrolls, a collection of Essene writings discovered from Qumran in 1947, the members of the sect are instructed "to be ruled by the primitive precepts in which (they) were first instructed until there shall come the Prophet and the Messiahs of Aaron and Israel."[13]

From other parts of the scrolls we know that the Messiahs of Aaron and Israel are a priestly and a royal figure and "the Prophet" is a figure like Moses expected on the basis of Deut. 18:15-19.[14] The evidence of a widespread Jewish expectation of three messianic figures is also preserved in the gospels. Thus in the Gospel of John the authorities in the Jerusalem temple send messengers to John the Baptist in order to find out what he claims himself to be. They conclude their inquiry with the question, "Why baptizest thou then, if thou be not the Christ (Messiah), nor Elijah, neither the Prophet?" (1:19-25). Two of the three figures mentioned here also appear in John 7:40-41, where people argue concerning Jesus: "Some of the people therefore when they heard him, said, 'This is surely the Prophet!' Others said, "He is the Messiah!" But others said, "Shall the Messiah come out of Galilee!" (See also John 6:14)

The figure of the Prophet was patterned on Moses and was sometimes identified with him, thus giving rise to an expectation of a second coming of Moses or of a coming of a second Moses.[15] This makes it certain that in the synoptic account of the transfiguration (Mark 9:2-4) where Jesus the Messiah appears in the company of Elijah and Moses we find presupposed the same expectation of three messianic figures that we find in the Dead Sea Scrolls and the Gospel of John.

This expectation of a trinity of messianic figures is based on certain passages in the Old Testament itself. But the Old Testament concerns itself largely with the pictures of the messianic future rather than with the agents through whom God will bring about that future. In the remaining chapters of this book we return to the Old Testament messianic prophecies, and the religious principles that inspired them, to see how far they are fulfilled through the work of the "messianic trinity." In this connection we find it valuable to maintain a distinction between universalist and purely nationalistic messianic hopes, a distinction to which we have already drawn attention in the two earlier chapters.

NOTES

1. See Adolf Harnack, *The Sayings of Jesus*, trans., J. R. Wilkinson (London, 1908). Rudolf Bultmann, *The History of the Synoptic Tradition*, tr. John March (Oxford, 1972).

2. The defeat of Satan is expected, for example, in a book called the *Assumption of Moses:* "And then His kingdom shall appear throughout all His creation, and then Satan shall be no more." (10). See also *Testament of Dan*, 5:31-64. Extraordinary healings and joy among the poor and the meek are predicted in *The Book of Isaiah:* "Then the eyes of the blind shall be opened, and the ears of the deaf shall be unstopped. Then shall the lame man leap as an hart, and the tongue of the dumb sing . . ." (Isa. 35:5-6). "The meek also shall increase their joy in the Lord, and the poor among men shall rejoice in the Holy One of Israel" (Isa. 29:19).

3. *Theology of the New Testament,* tr. F. Kendrich Grobel (Charles Scribner's Sons, New York, 1951, pp. 26-32.

4. *The Death of Christ,* 1969, pp. 31-125.

5. *Christologische Hoheitstitel: Ihre Geschichte Im Fruehen Christentum,* (Gottin Vandenhroek U. Ruprecht, 1963), pp. 13-53.

6. *The Son of Man in the Synoptic Tradition,* tr. By Dorothea M. Barton (1965), pp. 33-67.

7. *Jesus and the Son of Man* (Lutterworth Press, London 1964), pp. 186-209.

8. *The Foundation of New Testament Christonogy* (Charles Scribner's Sons, New York 1964), pp. 119-125.

9. See for details, A. Shafaat, *"Geber of the Qumran Scrolls and the Spirit-Paraclete of John,"* New Testament Studies, 1980.

10. A. Shafaat, *Jesus and the Messianic Figures,* unpublished, Chapter VII.

11. Bundahis XXX, 7, in *Sacred Books of the East,* gen. ed. F. Max Fuller.

12. Joseph Klausner, *The Messianic Idea in Israel,* tr. W. F. Stinespring (Macmillan Company, New York, 1955), p. 14.

13. G. Vermes, *The Dead Sea Scrolls in English* (Penguin Books, 1975), p. 87.

14. A more detailed discussion of the messianic expectations of the Qumran community may be found in A. Shafaat, *Jesus and the Messianic Figures,* unpublished.

15. Oscar Cullman, *Christology of the New Testament* (SCM, London, 1959), Chap. I.

Chapter IV

Fulfillment of Universalist Religious Hopes

By universalist messianic hopes we understand those Old Testament prophecies that foresee something good for mankind generally and not just its subjugation to the Israelites. These hopes may be for religious (spiritual and ethical) or material benefits. The present chapter is concerned with the fulfillment of hopes for the religious development of mankind, while fulfillment of hopes for material benefits of the messianic times will be the subject of the next chapter.

The fulfillment of universalist religious hopes begins with Christianity and consummates with Islam in a double sense. Firstly, these hopes, when considered as revelatory, are fulfilled in the sense that the religious principles revealed in them find their full development through the successive Christian and Islamic revelations. Secondly, they are fulfilled in the usual sense as predictions: their essential content as predictions is the hope for a global spread of the Old Testament religion, especially its monotheistic conception of God. This began with the coming of Christianity when the Old Testament, supplemented by ideas from non-Jewish religions and philosophies, began to be accepted as the word of God over a large part of the world. But Christianity carried around a confusing mixture of contradictory ideas in which the Old Testament views concerning even the most basic religious concepts, such as God and salvation, were modified beyond recognition.[1] The spread of Christianity and the circulation it gave to Old Testament ideas, however, did a valuable service in that it helped provide a context for the Islamic revelation which gave to the world a religious system, integrated and complete, and yet having greater affinity with the Old Testament religion than did Christianity. In this way Islam fulfills in a more satisfactory and complete manner the Old Testament prediction that its religion will one day be accepted all over the world. We will now deal with the above points in some detail.

I. Fulfillment By Completion of Revelation

The two main religious themes with which messianic prophecies are concerned are the conception of God and His Judgement. Both themes find their full development in Islam.

Conception of God

The Jewish concept of God, as we observed earlier, rose to great heights during the development of the Jewish religion, but in the Old Testament (see Chapter I) and in the subsequent tradition God retains, at least in practice, something of the character of a tribal idol. To this the Jews' peculiar attitude to their ancestry, race, and land throughout history bears testimony. The Jewish concept of God thus left one step to be taken to reveal a truly universal, unique, and transcendent God, namely, to break the idol of nationalism.

Christianity did not do that. Even Paul, the founder of Gentile Christianity, and the unknown writer of the fourth gospel, the most anti-semitic of New Testament writers, accept the absolute necessity for salvation to come somehow from Israel. The fourth gospel says quite simply: "It is from the Jews that salvation comes" (John 4:22). To be sure, the Christian Church became a global congregation in which all members tend to be equal - although it must be noted that the Christians have more then a normal inclination to divide into sects on national and racial lines - but the principle on which the Christian congregation was formed by no means negates the absolute religious nationalism of the Jews. The Church regarded itself as New Israel formed around the nucleus of a remnant fo old Israel (namely, Jesus and Jewish Christians). In principle, the Christian Church is nothing but people of various nations gathering together to share in the blessings and salvation that belong to the seed of Israel. This in principle amount to nothing more than adding converts to the community of Jews, an idea that was never alien to Jewish thinking, although the Jewish methods and approach have obviously not been as effective as those of the Christian Church. What is common between the Jews and the Christian Church is the view that those who are to have the knowledge of God and salvation must in some way link up with the race of Israel.

Nevertheless, the fact that the Christian Church quickly became an entirely Gentile congregation that had found reasons to be hostile to the Jews helped in practice to reduce emphasis on race. The idol of race was not broken, but receded further into the background. This gain, however, was more than offset by the deification of Jesus and the Holy Spirit, so that the Church ended up with a pantheon of three consciously professed gods and one idol buried in its subconscious. As a result of this, and of the mythological interpretations of the death of Christ, the concept of God sank far below the highest level that it had reached in the Jewish tradition.

Then came the Islamic revelation. It broke the idol of race and nationhood and corrected the Christian myths surrounding the death and person of Jesus. The revelation of one living, unique, universal, and transcendent God Who is fully involved in the individual and collective life of man was completed.

In the Qur'an there is a vivid awareness of mankind as one nation. Several times it emphasizes the common origin of all men and women.

> O mankind! Be mindful of your Lord Who created you from a single soul and from it created its mate, and (then) scattered countless men and women (like seeds) from the two of them. . . .
>
> (4:1)

> Mankind was but one nation and then they differed.
>
> (10:19; cf. 2:213)

To be sure, mankind is divided into nations and tribes, but this division is only for convenience.

> O mankind! We created you from a single pair of parents and made you into nations and tribes so that you may know one another. But surely the best among you in the sight of Allah is the most righteous of you (49:13).

Jews are not specially dear to God (62:6) and nowhere in the Qur'an do Arabs replace the Jews as Allah's special people. To be sure, the families of Abraham and 'Imran were chosen by Allah over all mankind (3:33) but this means only that the three messianic messengers, John, Jesus, and Muhammad (AS) and the most favoured of women, Mary, came from these families.[2] Otherwise no nation or tribe has a monopoly over knowledge of Allah or salvation. Revelation is a bounty of Allah that He grants to whom He wills (3:73) and in fact in every nation there have been prophets, messengers, or warners:

> To every nation have we sent a messenger (with the message): Turn to Allah and turn away from evil (16:36).

There has been no nation but a warner has passed among them (35:24).

Salvation too is not restricted to any particular group, not even to Muslims. To be sure Muhammad has been sent as a messenger and mercy to all mankind (4:79-80, 25:1, 3:28) and messengers are sent to be obeyed by Allah's permission (4:64). Those who choose to become his enemies are cutting themselves off from salvation (108:3). In principle, true faith backed by fitting deeds, wherever it may be found, will lead to salvation:

Surely any among the Muslims, Jews, Sabians, and Christians who believe in Allah and the hereafter and act constructively will have no fear nor shall they grieve (5:69).

And whosoever does good works, whether male or female, and has faith, will enter Paradise and will not be wronged in any way (4:124).

And (the Jews and Christians) say, "None shall enter Paradise except a Jew or a Christian". Those are just their vain desires. Say, "Bring your proof for this, if you are truthful". Nay - whosoever commits himself fully to Allah and does good, he will be rewarded by Allah; and there shall be no fear upon him nor shall he grieve (2:111-112).

Only those who set up partners with Allah that are believed to share in some way His "Godhead" are certainly condemned to damnation (4:48, 116-117). Just as genuine faith is rewarded wherever it may be found, this unforgivable sin will lead to damnation wherever it may be found. For example, the trinitarian Christians, who deify Jesus have no hope of salvation (5:57-76) even though they may at the same time somehow affirm the unity of God (cf. 3:64).

A Jewish or Christian mind may ask here what the need for Muhammad (AS) is if one can find God and salvation without him. The answer is that the function of the prophet Muhammad (AS) is precisely to reveal this universal and unique God, Whose Knowledge and salvation is not limited to any race or congregation and is not affected through only a specific person or event. He is needed to make the knowledge of God universal and safeguard it from the various ways it had been corrupted time and again before him. In doing so he completes the revelation and is destined to perform the most momentous function of forming mankind into a single nation serving the same God, the only true God that there is. But while the process toward this destiny of Muhammad (AS) is going on, the possibility of men outside of Islam finding true faith and leading good lives and therefore being saved is not excluded.

Allah, the one true God, the God of all mankind, is, of course, the central theme of the Qur'anic revelation. We place before the reader a very short selection of Qur'anic passages that tell us what kind of God is revealed in the Qur'an.

Say: Allah is Unique
Allah, the Self-Existing
He has not fathered anyone
nor was He fathered,
and there is nothing comparable to Him (112).

Allah! There is no deity except Him,
the Living, the Eternal!
Slumber does not overtake Him, nor does sleep.
What the Heavens hold and what the Earth holds belongs to Him.
Who is there to intercede with Him except with His permission?
(2:225)

They have set up jinns as associates with Allah although He created them.
They have even dared to impute sons and daughters to Him without basis in knowledge.
Glory be to Him! Exalted is He over what they attribute to Him (6:100).

No vision can grasp Him, but His grasp is over all vision (6:103).

Allah is He who splits the seed and the kernel, He brings the living from the dead, and is the One who brings the dead from the living (6:95).

Have they adopted other patrons instead of Allah?
He is the (only) Patron; He revives the dead.
He is capable of everything (42:9).

He is the One who accepts repentance from His servants and overlooks (many of their) evil deeds; but He knows anything that you do (42:25).

And it is We who created man and We know what evil his soul suggests to him. For we are nearer to him than his jugular vein (50:16).

When My servants ask you (O Prophet) concerning Me, I am near. I listen to the prayer of everyone when he calls to Me ... (2:186)

If Allah supports you there is no-one who can overcome you, while if He should forsake you, who is there to support you? On God let the believers rely (3:160).

I afflict anyone I wish with My torment, while My mercy embraces everything ... (7:156)

Say: If you have (any) love for God, then follow me; Allah will then love you and forgive you your offences. Allah is forgiving, merciful (3:31).

These and numerous other passages[3] show that in the Qur'an God is an utterly sublime and self-sufficient Being who has no partners and is unique and transcendent. He is in complete control of everything. He is near to the affairs of men and He communicated with them through numerous messengers time and again. He is extremely kind and can be loved, relied upon, and taken as a friend and protector, and indeed He is really the only helper and friend. He is everywhere and in everything, for everything is a Divine sign that contributes to man's knowledge of Him.

Allah's Judgement of Men

It should now be clear that the idea of one God, who is at once universal and personal, which was partly developed in the Old Testament and improved by Christianity in one direction but corrupted in another, reaches its full development in Islam. We now turn to the second of the two basic religious themes, the development of which through Jewish, Christian, and Islamic religions we set out to consider , namely, the concept of Allah's judgement of men.

In the Old Testament there seems to be no conception of an eschatological, suprahistorical age when men will be raised, judged, and either taken to paradise or to hell, such as we find in Christianity and Islam. Everything in store for man is conceived there in historical this-wordly terms. Mythological and symbolical language in the messianic prophecies may seem to suggest that the prophets have in mind a world wholly different from this world of ours, but such language was part and parcel of the apparatus of ancient poetic and religious writings. A closer analysis of the prophecies leads one to the conclusion drawn by Mowinckel,[4] namely, that the "national and this-wordly element remains the heart of the future hope throughout the entire Old Testament period." More specifically, the Old Testament hopes for conditions of perfect peace, righteousness, prosperity, and happiness through the establishment of God's kingly rule on earth in the form of an everlasting world-hegemony of Israel and her Davidic ruler.

But in history, world hegemonies do not last, much less those that bring "perfect" conditions. So, like the Persians and under their influence, it later began to be realized by many Jewish writers that this world might never offer the lasting and total peace, happiness, and righteousness expected earlier, but that for these expectations to be fulfilled this old world and its entire order must break up and give way to a new world. The first century apocalypse, 4 Ezra, expressed the idea in these words:

> ... the age is hastening swiftly to its end. For it will not be able to bring the things that have been promised to the righteous in their appointed times, because this age is full of sadness and infirmities. For the evil ... has been sown ... If therefore ... the place where the evil has been sown does not pass away, the field where good has been sown will not come (4:26-28).

Along with the belief in a new age, wholly different from the present and free from evil and suffering, there also entered into some Jewish writings the belief in resurrection of the dead. Some of the other eastern religious traditions were already led to this belief by the concern for justice and judgement common to all religions. In the Old Testament, where the resurrection of the dead is not taught, the justice of God operated solely through social and political happenings: the heathen, for example, will be judged by their political defeat and subservience to Yahweh's people; the sinners among the Jews will die by the sword during the course of history. This concept of justice is not satisfactory, since it leaves the possibility of an individual getting away with sin without being punished; for until Yahweh brings about the expected defeat of the worshippers of other gods, many a heathen and Jewish sinner may complete his or her life in relatively greater comfort and happiness, while many a righteous Jew may live and die in suffering. The belief in the resurrection solves the difficulty.

But since they do not have any roots in the Old Testament tradition, these new ideas of resurrection and a new age were not universally and fully accepted by the Jews, and wherever they were accepted they combined with the older messianic tradition of the Old Testament period to produce only a more uncertain and confused picture of the future. For despite the acceptance of a transcendental, suprahistorical world after this present world "it was never forgotten that the starting point for the future hope was faith in the restoration of Israel as a free people among other nations, on this earth, in the land of Canaan. Thus there persisted in eschatology an unresolved tension between those elements that were political, national, and this-worldy, and those universal and transcendental elements that belonged to the world beyond."[5]

Christianity did not resolve the tension and, in fact, increased the confusion between this world and the other. To a certain degree the tension seems to be present even in the reported sayings of Jesus himself; he generally looks forward to a future transcendent age, resurrection, and judgement, but a few of his sayings suggest paradoxically the presence, through him, of a suprahistorical age within the historical age. Jesus' sayings, as far as they can be dug out from the mass of the gospel tradition, also leave painfully unclear the role he saw for himself in this world or the other.[6]

But it was after Jesus' departure from this world, when the Church attempted to define his role more definitely, that the tension between this world and the other, the here and the hereafter, produces almost total confusion. The first generation of Christians came to believe that the Man or the Son of Man whom Jesus expected as a future messianic figure was Jesus himself and that he would come back on the clouds of heaven in the capacity of Man within their lifetime. Speaking in the name of Jesus, "prophets" in the Church uttered such words:

When they persecute you in one town run away to another. Verily I say unto you that you will not have finished all the towns of Israel before you will see the Son of Man coming (Matt. 10:23).

I tell you, there are some standing here who will not taste death before they see the Reign of God (the future age) come with power (Mark 9:1).

But when the first generation of Christians passed away without seeing the coming of the Son of Man, the view began to be held by many that Jesus, in his first coming, had already ushered in the new, eschato-logical age, either by his death and resurrection (John 16) or by his works and words (John 14-15). Mainstream Christianity accepted this view when it included the Gospel of John in its canon, but only alongside the opposite view in the weightier, older tradition, which preached a thoroughly future-oriented eschatology. This inevitably resulted in the paradoxical view that the eschatological, suprahistorical age is somehow already present in history but that it will also somehow become more eschatological with the second coming of Jesus. A great deal of modern Christian theology is engaged in debating solutions to this paradox, but clearly a paradox embedded in the New Testament cannot be solved on the basis of the New Testament. A fresh revelation is needed.

Thus just as Jewish and Christian traditions leave a certain confusion between God and man or God and nation, they also leave some confu-sion between the eschatological and the historical elements in future expectations. And just as the Islamic revelation removes the first confu-sion, so also it removes the second.

The Qur'an presents a clear and consistent picture of the future of man. It expects resurrection followed by the judgement of men before Allah and their division into two classes: The people of Paradise and the people of Hell. This division is final and eternal. There will be no death. But all this is strictly in the future. At present our existence is historical existence of the same kind as men have known since Adam and will con-tinue to know till the resurrection. In particular, total and lasting peace and harmony or perfect righteousness or happiness never known before will not be known in future history - the devil has been given respite till the day of resurrection (7:14-15) and hardship and ease go together (94:5); conflict among men is ordained for their earthly existence (7:24-25). Neither is full judgement possible in history, but the victories and defeats in conflict among people and the rise and fall of nations point to certain religious and moral principles (103; 6:11).

This world and this age, however, are not without purpose (21:16, 3:190). Allah does have a purpose *within* history and man is His primary agent or vicegerent (2:30), a role in which he has been often helped through prophetic revelation. But divine purpose in history cannot be set down in a detailed once-and-for-all formulation in the manner of Ezekiel's vision of the Jerusalem of messianic times (Ezek. 40-48). It unfolds in history without being fully known at any time. When men do perform their divinely ordained role as instruments of God's purpose in history they do so simply by following at any time the path shown to them directly and individually,[7] or collectively through a prophet. They have little idea where destiny is taking them (31:34). The divine purpose in history, which messianic prophecy attempts to express in concrete terms, is realized through divine revelation. Fulfillment of messianic prophecy is in fact the coming of certain revelations. John, Jesus, and Muhammad (AS) are therefore presented in the Qur'an as bearers of revelation or messengers of God, like other messengers known to history before them, and not in the manner of the Gospels as figures who live and carry out their mission according to a blueprint extracted from some messianic predictions.[8] They "fulfill" earlier expectations (see Chap. III), but they do so as successive bearers of revelation who came at crucial stages of history. In the case of Prophet Muhammad (SAWS) this comes out quite clearly in the following verse: "Whether you believe in it (the revelation brought by the Prophet) or not, it is certain that those who possessed knowledge before it fall on their face in humble prostation when it is recited to them. And they say, Glory to our Lord, Truly has the promises of our Lord been fulfilled" (17:107-108).

According to this verse, what those with knowledge were promised aforetime finds fulfillment in nothing other than a revelation, a revelation that makes men bow to their true Lord and thus brings them in touch with the reality of their existence (59:19). From this revelation everything good that mankind is destined to get will follow. Every earlier prophecy that can be fulfilled will find fulfillment. For a prophecy that can be fulfilled is nothing but a statement about the potential of life and faith and this potential can be fully realized through a revelation which brings men in touch with their Lord and hence with themselves.

II. Fulfillment Through Universal Expansion of Islam

We have seen above that messianic prophecies when regarded as the revelation of certain religious principles find their fulfillment through Islam (with Christianity playing a preparatory role) in the sense that these principles find a complete, consistent, and fully developed form in Islam. We shall now show how Islam fulfills the universalist religious type of messianic prophecies when we regard them as predications.

Messianic hopes of a religious type fall into three categories: 1) those that look forward to universal acceptance of Yahweh, the God of Jacob, who is also the Lord and Creator of the whole universe; 2) universal acceptance of other elements of the Old Testament religion; and 3) establishment of the (rebuilt) temple in Jerusalem as a house of prayer for all nations.

And They Shall Know The Lord

Among the most remarkable predictions of the first category is one found in the following passage from First Isaiah:

> In that day shall five cities in the land of Egypt speak the language of Canaan, and swear to the Lord of hosts; one shall be called, The city of destruction. In that day shall there be an altar to the Lord in the midst of the land of Egypt, and a pillar at the border thereof to the Lord. And it shall be for a sign and for a witness unto the Lord of hosts in the land of Egypt: for they shall cry unto the Lord because of the oppressors, and He shall send them a saviour, and a great one, and he shall deliver them. And the Lord shall be known to Egypt, and the Egyptians shall know the Lord in that day, and shall do sacrifice and oblation; yea, they shall vow a vow unto the Lord, and perform it. And the Lord shall smite Egypt; He shall smite and heal it; and they shall return even to the Lord, and He shall be entreated by them and shall heal them.
>
> In that day shall there be highway out of Egypt to Assyria, and the Assyrian shall come into Egypt, and the Egyptian into Assyria, and the Egyptians shall serve with the Assyrians. In that day shall Israel be the third with Egypt, and with Assyria, even a blessing in the midst of the land: when the Lord of hosts shall bless, saying, Blessed be Egypt my people, and Assyria the work of my hands, and Israel mine inheritance.
>
> (Isa. 19:18-25)

Egypt and Assyria were the two superpowers that influenced the politics of Palestine in Isaiah's time. During the prophet's long ministry (about 40 years) they at times attacked parts of Palestine while at other times they fought with each other. This explains why Isaiah mentions only Israel, Assyria, and Egypt, despite the fact that his vision seems to be universal. But the prediction itself does not spring from a knowledge of the political situation of the time and of the direction the political events might take, for there was no indication at the time that Egyptians, Assyrians, and Israelites might join in the worship of one and the same God. The prediction springs rather from pure faith and hope.

The prediction found a most amazing fulfillment in Islam,[9] through which the Egyptians came to know and accept the God of Jacob and Moses. In commemoration of Abraham's sacrifice of his only son they make sacrifices to Allah, and as Muslims they were united with the inhabitants of Palestine and Isaiah's Assyria. Prophet Muhammad (SAWS) may well be described as "a saviour, and a great one" sent to the Egyptians.

Ironically, it is the Jews themselves who stand in the way of a more complete fulfillment of Isaiah's vision, for they refuse to join the Egyptians and other Middle Eastern people in the worship of the God of Jacob, the Lord and Creator of the world, simply because the way He has chosen for establishing in the world His exclusive worship does not put the Jews in a leading or dominating position. In an attempt to relive the politics of more than two thousand years ago, they have even injected themselves into the area, causing one of the most serious, difficult, and dangerous conflicts in history. But in the spirit of Isaiah's faith, I too venture to hope that all this is temporary and one day the Jews will realize that Islam provides the only meaningful and constructive way of fulfilling the Old Testament hopes.

The hope for a universal acceptance and worship of the God of Abraham and Jacob, or, as I would like to put it, Allah, the true God who communicated with Abraham and Jacob, is found in the books of most of the prophets from Isaiah onward: First and Second Isaiah, Micah, Zephaniah, Habbakuk, Jeremiah, First and Second Zachariah, Joel, Malachi and the Psalms. We quote from these books some more passages in which this hope is voiced:

> The Lord will be terrible unto them (Moab, Ammon etc.): for He will famish all the gods of the earth; and men shall worship Him, every one from his place, even all the isles of the heathen (Zeph. 2:11).

> For then will I turn to the peoples
> A pure language,
> That they may all call upon the name of the Lord
> To serve Him with one consent (Zeph. 3:9).

In this last passage, the original Hebrew behind the phrase "with one consent" literally means "one shoulder", that is, "shoulder to shoulder" or "side by side".[10] By "pure language" the prophet must have meant a divinely standardized, incorruptible, expression of religious matters. Such an expression is provided by the Qur'anic revelation, which has been preserved for all times in its original form and language. The vision in Zephaniah's passage finds a literal fulfillment in the spectacle of Muslims from various races and nations praying shoulder to shoulder, using the same language in every part of the world.

Among other passages where universal establishment of the worship of One God is predicted are the following:

> I have sworn by myself, the word is gone out of my mouth in righteousness and shall not return, That unto me every knee shall bow, every tongue shall swear (Isa. 45:23).

> Be still, and know that I am God: I will be exalted among the heathen, I will be exalted in the earth (Psalm 46:10).

These promises of Allah are coming true through Islam. In more and more parts of the earth, and among more and more nations of the world, the true God who communicated with, among other men, Abraham, Jacob, and Moses, is worshipped and glorified as never before. Sentences like "Allah is greater than all," "All glory is due to Allah," "In the name of Allah, the Most Gracious, the Most Merciful," "There is no deity but Allah," are used constantly by Muslims the world over to remind everyone just who is to be exalted and worshipped by mankind.

Christianity also has taken the name of the Old Testament God into every part of the earth, but it has so confused Him with the man Jesus born in Palestine around 4 B.C. that very little is left of Him. Still, as we noted earlier, Christianity made a valuable contribution by preparing the way for the Islamic revelation of a truly transcendent God.

And the Isles Shall Wait for His Law

We now turn to some passages that hope not just for the universal acceptance and worship of the God of Moses and the prophets, but also for a wide acceptance of other elements of the Old Testament religion. The most famous of these passages is the first of the so-called Servant Songs:

> Behold My servant whom I uphold (strengthen); Mine elect, in whom My soul delighteth; I have filled him with My spirit and he shall bring justice to the nations. He shall not cry, nor lift up, nor cause his voice to be heard in the street. A bruised reed shall he not break and the flickering lamp shall he not put out. He shall

bring forth true justice. He shall not fail nor be discouraged till he has set justice in the earth and the isles shall wait for his law. Thus saith God the Lord, He that created the heavens, and stretched them out; He that spread forth the earth, and all that is found there; He that giveth breath unto the people upon it, and spirit to them that walk therein: I, the Lord, have called thee in righteousness, and will hold thine hand, and will keep thee and give thee for a covenant of the people, for a light to the nations, to open the blind eyes, to bring out those who sit in dark prisons. I am the Lord thy God and My will I do not give to another, neither My praise to graven images. Behold, things formerly declared have come to pass, and new things do I declare, even before they begin to happen. Sing unto the Lord a new song, and His praise from the end of the earth, ye that sail the sea and all that is therein; the isles and those that inhabit them. Let the wilderness and its cities lift up their voices, the villages that Kedar doth inhabit.

see p. 44 ✓

Let the inhabitants of Sela sing, let them shout from the tops of the mountains.

Let them give glory to the Lord, and let them declare His praise in the island. (Isa. 42:1-12)

The title "servant" used in the opening verse of the song can be applied by Second Isaiah to a person (Isa. 45:1, Isa. 53) or the people of Israel (Isa. 45:4) who are often referred to in the singular. But in the present passage the reference is almost certainly to Israel. The idea briefly is that God has chosen the Israelites (hence reference to them in verse 1 as "Mine elect") to perform a service to Him (hence the designation "My servant"). This service is to establish throughout the world, even in remote isles, the principles of justice and the divine law with which Israelites have been entrusted (vv. 1-4), especially unshared glorification and worship of the God who created the universe and life (v.5) and for whom images cannot be substituted. (v.8). For this service God has kept the Israelites, so that the light of God's religion may spread among all the nations and they may come out of darkness to light (vv. 6-7). This will happen without any loud propaganda or any other effort on the part of the Israelites (v.3).

The divine law and principles of justice whose establishment is being predicted in the song should not be taken to be as well-defined as, for example, the universal acceptance of the whole of the Pentateuch or the Old Testament, since the Jewish religion had lost the detailed revelation to Moses and did not take any such standard form until after Second Isaiah. Nor should it be taken as completely unrelated to Jewish beliefs and practices; for Second Isaiah expects such Jewish laws as the prohibition against eating the flesh of swine to be observed by all those who will be saved (66:17).

The predicted global spread of the religion preserved by the Israelites during their long troubled history has come to pass through Islam to an impressive degree. Monotheism, first given expression in Second Isaiah among the books of the Old Testament, has been accepted through Islam in a large part of the world. Many of the laws found in the Torah, such as stoning for adultery, "an eye for an eye" etc., are part of the legal practice of Islam, though modified by mercy, and many popular customs continue, such as circumcision and many dietary and other regulations. The idea of an extremely merciful and forgiving God found in the Old Testament and emphasized in Christianity is also fully present is Islam, as also is the concept of a religious truth and justice beyond laws and regulations. Here I am emphasizing what Islam has in common with the Old Testament religion, but of course Islam goes much further than the Jewish religion. For one thing, whereas the sources of Jewish religion contain both formal and essential contradictions, Islam gave the world an integrated system. Secondly, many of the elements of the Old Testament religion accepted in Islam are found there in a fully developed form. But the fact relevant to us here is that Islam has greater affinity with the religion of Second Isaiah than any other religion and its spread in every corner of the world represents a remarkable fulfillment of the hope found in the first Servant Song.

Indeed, it is hard to think of any better way of fulfilling that hope. The Jews may expect to see the hope fulfilled through a worldwide acceptance of their religion in its entirety(i.e. the Old Testament and the tradition built on it later) but, as we noted above, this is far from what Second Isaiah meant. Moreover, after having been developed among, and for a long time remaining restricted to, a particular people, the Jewish religion had acquired a character that made it unsuited to become a global religion in its entirety: it became too deeply rooted in the history of that particular people, became too nationalistic, and, since developed by a large number of persons over a long period of time, had accumulated all kinds of contradictions. Only after a creative process of integration, of restating essential religious truth in universal terms, simplifying the laws, clearing a lot of inessential and circumstantial details, and removing contradictions, could the Old Testament religion meaningfully be taken to all nations. And this is what Islam achieved after Christianity had prepared the way for it.

Even the fact that Islam originated from among the Ishmaelites and not the Israelites is consistent with the spirit of the Song. For the statement in verse 3 that the predicted global spread of the religion entrusted to the Israelites will come about without any propaganda or other type of effort on their part allows, and even demands, that the means for the fulfillment of the prediction originated from outside the nation of Israel. Moreover, Second Isaiah is quite willing to regard Cyrus, the Persian king, as God's servant and messiah (Isa. 45:1) through whom God carried out His purpose and therefore would have no objection to see in an Arab the instrument of the fulfillment of its hopes.

In verses 10-11, where the inhabitants of all the far-off places of the earth are invited to sing a new song to the Lord, Sela and other villages inhabited by Kedar are mentioned specifically, as if these places have a special reason to rejoice in the coming universal glorification of the Lord. Whether the choice was made out of a genuine glimpse of the future in the Islamic age without the prophet fully realizing the implication of what he was seeing, or whether this is coincidence, the fact is that Sela and Kedar are associated with the Arabs. Sela was an Arabian town and Kedar was a tribe of Ishmaelites descending from a son of Ishmael with the same name (Gen 25:12-13). Independent tradition has it that Prophet Muhammad (SAWS) belonged to Kedar.

In view of the extraordinary fulfillment that the first Servant Song finds in the work of Prophet Muhammad (SAWS), it is fitting that the Song is one of the few, if not the only, Old Testament passage applied to the Prophet in the sources of Islam. In several traditions, the song in Isaiah 42 is quoted in free and summarized forms. The clearest quotation is found in the following tradition.

'Ata son of Yasar related that he met Abdullah son of Amr son of al-'As and asked him to tell him of the description of God's messenger as given in the Torah. He agreed, swearing by God that the Torah certainly contains part of the description of the prophet in the Qur'an: "O prophet, We have sent you as a witness, a bearer of good tidings, and a warner" (33:45), and a guard for common people. The description of the Prophet in the Torah is as follows:

YOU ARE MY SERVANT and my messenger; I HAVE CALLED YOU the one who trusts, NOT HARSH OR ROUGH, NOR LOUD-VOICED

IN THE STREETS. He will not repulse evil with evil, but will pardon and forgive, and GOD WILL NOT TAKE HIM TILL HE USES HIM TO STRAIGHTEN THE CROOKED CREED AND PEOPLE MAY SAY THERE IS NO DEITY BUT GOD: AND OPENS THEREBY BLIND EYES, DEAF EARS, AND HARDENED HEARTS.

Bukhari transmitted it. Darimi also gives something to the same effect on the authority of 'Ata who gave as his authority Ibn Salam *(Mishkat al-Musabih* book 24, Chap. 18, Section I; see also Chap. 18, Section II and Chap. 20, Section III).

The portions in capitals in the above tradition are clearly a summary of the song of Isaiah 42. In other traditions a freer summary is made by some Jews when they accepted Islam in the presence of the Prophet (AS).

Mine House Shall Be Called the House of Prayer for All People

In view of the hope that all or many nations will one day worship the God of Jacob and give acceptance to the Jewish religion in general, the hopes are hardly surprising in the Old Testament that Jewish holy places, Jerusalem and its temple, will be accepted as sacred by people the world over and become the object of their pilgrimages. This hope is found in many passages, of which we quote two:

> Even them (non-Jewish people) will I bring to my holy mountain, and make them joyful in my house of prayer: their burnt offerings and their sacrifices shall be accepted upon Mine altar; for Mine house shall be called an house of prayer for all people. (Isa. 56:7)

> And many nations shall come, and say, Come, and let us go up to the mountain of the Lord, and to the house of the God of Jacob; and He will teach us of His ways, and we will walk in His paths: for the law shall go forth out of Zion, and the word of the Lord from Jerusalem.
>
> (Isa. 2:3, Micah 4:2)

The hope that Jerusalem will become a holy city for the people the world over has been fulfilled through Christianity and Islam. Hundreds of millions of Christians and Muslims today hold Jerusalem a sacred city and many of them visit it as pilgrims.

The words "their burnt offerings and their sacrifices shall be accepted at Mine altar" in the first passage should be interpreted loosely to mean that people from other nations will pray in the temple. This prediction has come true through Islam: as the Mosque of Omar, the Jerusalem temple has truly become today "the house of prayer for all nations". It may be instructive at this point briefly to recall the history of Jerusalem and its temple.

The earliest recorded masters of Jerusalem were the Egyptians. In the 14th century B.C. the city's ruler, abdi-Kheba asked his overlord for help against the incursions of the Hapiru or Habiru, most probably the same as the Hebrews of the Bible. It was in about 1000 B. C. that King David captured the city and made it the capital of the joint kingdom of Judah and Israel of which he was the founder. His illustrious successor, King Solomon, built the temple on the site of an ancient non-Jewish shrine. In the early 6th centry B.C. the city and the temple were destroyed completely by the Babylonians, who found no other way to deal with the seditions of the Jews. About a generation later the temple was rebuilt under the more favorable policies of the Persian emperor Cyrus, then overlord of Palestine. Some centuries later it was the Romans' turn to experience the difficulties of dealing with the absolute nationalism of the Jews and they too found no other way but to destroy Jewish institutions as completely as they could, including the temple in Jerusalem. The temple was finally rebuilt as the Dome of the Rock by the Muslims in the period from 688-691, but this time it was built as a house of the God of Jacob where people from all nations and races came for His worship. The Muslim-built house of prayer has stood for many more centuries than any before in recorded history.

Isaiah's prediction that "the law shall go forth out of Zion, and the word of the Lord from Jerusalem" also has great potential for fulfillment. In considering the sacred history of Palestine and Jerusalem in which two billion Jews, Christians, and Muslims are involved, it is natural to expect that when the atmosphere created by the present phase of Jewish nationalism changes, major Judaeo - Christian - Islamic institutes of religious learning will be built in these places and religious students from all over the world will go there for their studies. In the final stage of the fulfillment of the universalist messianic prophecies, when the Egyptians, Assyrians, and Israelites will join in Islam to worship the one true God, Allah, (see our comments on Isa. 19:16-25 above), these institutions may be retained to perform a new function.

NOTES

1. The Central Christian dogma of a trinity of three persons in one godhead one of whom becomes incarnate to be crucified for the salvation of the world, is totally alien to the religion of the Old Testament, as is also the important Pauline conclusion that "a man is justified by faith alone apart from works of law" (Rom 3:28). This principle completely negates the important position the law occupies in the Old Testament; and it conflicts violently with another statement in the New Testament itself: "You see that a man is justified by works and not by faith alone" (James 2:24).

2. This is shown by the way verse 3:33 serves as an introduction for the stories of the births of Mary, John, and Jesus (AS), and is then followed by a reference to the relationship between Muhammad (SAWS) and Abraham (AS).

3. See T. B. Irving, et. al., *The Quran: Basic Teachings* (The Islamic Foundation, Leicerter, 1979), for a more extensive selection of the Qur'anic verses on the subject of God.

4. Mowinckel, *He That Cometh*, trans, G. W. Anderson (Basil Blackwell, Oxford, 1956), p. 149.

5. Mowinckel, op.cit., p. 267.

6. A. Shafaat, *Jesus and The Messianic Figures*, unpublished, Chaps. III and VI.

7. Direct and personal guidance from God to individuals generally and not just to prophets is frequently mentioned in the Qur'an. It is the object of the oft-repeated prayer: "Show us the right path, the path of those whom You have favored and not of those who earned Your wrath, neither of those who have gone astray" (1:5-7). Personal guidance is also mentioned in such Qur'anic passages as 87:2-3: "(The Lord) who creates and shapes, and who destines and then guides (to that destiny)" and 91:7-10: "By the soul and Him who gave it order; And inspired it concerning what is wrong for it and what is right for it; He is indeed successful who causes it to grow; And he is indeed a failure who corrupts it."

8. In contrast to the Gospels (see Chap. II) the Qur'an shuns mention of specific messianic predictions. The only specific reference in the Qur'an to a messianic prediction in connection with the Prophet Muhammad (SAWS) is the reference to Jesus' prophecy about a Messenger Ahmad (meaning Muhammad or Admirable). In connection with John there is no such reference, while in the case of Jesus the names "Messiah," which retains none of its original connotations, is the only link with the messianic tradition.

9. Whenever we note fulfillment of a messianic prophecy as a prediction, we do so with all those observations in mind that were made in Chap. II concerning the interpretation of prophecies. In particular, we never imply that the messianic prophecy in question was necessarily written with a clear foreknowledge of that particular event in which we see its fulfillment, but rather we attribute this fulfillment to the soundness of the logic and profoundness of the religious insight which we believe inspired the prophecy.

10. Joseph Klausner, *The Messianic Idea in Israel*, trans. W. F. Stinespring (London), p. 86.

Chapter V

Fulfillment of Materialistic Hopes

I. Hopes

Numerous messianic passages in the Old Testament promise an extraordinary improvement in the material condition of man. They foresee peace among nations and harmony in nature, abundance of food, increase in population, elimination of sickness, etc. The following famous passage is found in the books of both Isaiah and Micah:

> And he shall judge among many people, and rebuke strong nations afar off; and they shall beat their swords into plowshares, and their spears into pruninghooks: nation shall not lift up sword against nation, neither shall they learn war any more. But they shall sit every man under his vine and under his fig tree; and none shall make them afraid. (Micah 4:3-4; see also Isa. 2:4)

Not only will there be peace among nations but the whole of nature will experience an extraordinary harmony:

> And the wolf shall dwell with the lamb,
> And the leopard shall lie down with the kid,
> And the calf and the young lion and fatling together;
> And a little child shall lead them . . .
> . . . For the earth shall be full of the knowledge of the Lord
> As the waters cover the sea. (Isa. 11:6-9)

The knowledge of God, according to the last verse, is the source of peace and harmony. The next passage also states that peace and other materialistic benefits shall spring from revelation (from "spirit poured upon us from on high"). There is also a close relation between peace (both inner and external) justice and righteousness:

Because the palaces shall be forsaken; the multitude of the city shall be left; the forts and towers shall be for dens forever, a joy of wild asses, a pasture of flocks. Until the spirit be poured upon us from on high, and the wilderness be a fruitful field, and the fruitful field be counted for a forest. Then justice shall dwell in the wilderness and righteousness in the fruitful field. And the work of righteousness shall be peace; and the effect of righteousness quietness and assurance for ever.   (Isa. 32:14-17)

Along with peace, justice, and righteousness there will be extraordinary prosperity. The soil will be surprisingly productive:

Behold, the days come, saith the Lord (when food will grow so fast) that the plowman shall overtake the reaper, and the treader of grapes him that soweth seed; and the mountains shall drop sweet wine, and all the hills shall melt. (Amos 9:13)

The diseases presently incurable will be eliminated:

Then the eyes of the blind shall be opened,
And the ears of the deaf unstopped.
Then shall the lame man leap as an hart,
and the tongue of the dumb sing.
For in the wilderness shall waters break out,
and a stream in the desert.
And the parched ground shall become a pool,
and the thirsty land springs of water . . .
                              (Isa. 35:5-7)

No wonder, then, that there will be a great increase in population and desolate lands will be inhabited:

And I will multiply men upon you, all the house of Israel, even all of it; and the cities shall be inhabited and waste shall be builded. (Ezek. 36:10; see also Isa. 49:19)

Thus saith the Lord God, in the day that I shall have cleansed you from all your iniquities I will also cause you to dwell in the cities, and the wastes shall be builded. And the desolate land shall be tilled, whereas it lay desolate in the sight of all that passed by. And they shall say, This land that was desolate is become like the garden of Eden; and the waste and desolate cities are become fenced, and are inhabited.   (Ezek. 36:33-35)

Many of the materialistic benefits are often mentioned with the prophet's attention focused on the Israelites and their land. But it is fair to say that prophets like First and Second Isaiah who could see salvation coming to the Egyptians and Assyrians and even "unto the ends of the earth" (Isa. 49:6) would allow these benefits to be shared by the whole world. This is also explicitly stated in the following passage:

And in this mountain shall the Lord of hosts make unto all nations a feast of fat things, a feast of wines on the lees, of fat things full of marrow, of wines on the lees well refined. And he will destroy in this mountain the covering of sorrow cast over all people, and the vail of misery spread over all nations. He will swallow up death in victory . . . (Isa. 25:6-8)

Of course, even in Second Isaiah the best fruits of messianic times will be reserved for the Israelites:

Thy heart shall throb and be enlarged
Because the abundance of the sea shall be turned unto thee.
The wealth of the nations shall come unto thee.
The caravan of camels shall cover thee.
And of the young camels of Midian and Ephal,
All coming from Sheba;
They shall bring gold and frankincense,
And shall proclaim the praises of the Lord.

(Isa. 60:5-6)

II. Fulfillment

To the extent that materialistic messianic expectations call for perfect and eternal peace, harmony, and prosperity, they have not been fulfilled. According to the Qur'an they cannot be fulfilled in history, for the devil has been given respite till the end of history (7:14-15), conflict is inherent in man's situation on earth because of his imperfection (2:36)[1] and with ease goes hardship (94:5-6). But short of perfection and the eternal there is certainly a potential in human life in the direction of all these material hopes, and this potential is being realized in history.

Through modern science some of the materialistic hopes have been fulfilled in a literal way. Today it is possible to grow plants for food bigger and faster than they used to grow in earlier times. Men live longer and healthier lives and the population of the world is many times more than it used to be in the Old Testament times. Deserts have been supplied with water and desolate places have been inhabited. Medical science has found cures for many diseases previously incurable, eliminated some others, and who knows whether one day in the future it will not find remedies for the blind, the deaf, the dumb, and the lame.

Some of the passages quoted above (Isa. 11:6-9; 32:14-17) suggest that the materialistic benefits of messianic times will spring from revelation ("the knowledge of the Lord' or the "spirit poured upon us"). Indeed it seems to be true that the fulfillment of many materialistic expectations, though more directly made possible by science, is ultimately a fruit of the revelations brought by the "messianic trinity." For it is a fact of history that modern science is a product of the civilization that came to be founded on Islam and it is probable that at a late stage Christianity too played a positive role in the development of science and technology. The demonstration of both these claims will naturally require covering a rather large area in the history of ideas, of which it is not possible to give a full account in the present work. We simply have to content ourselves with brief arguments and a partial survey of Muslim achievements in science (see Appendix II).

Science as an activity concerned with perceiving phenomena, correlating them by the use of reason and intuition and, whenever possible, applying the knowledge so acquired to solve the problems of life, is almost as old as human civilization. It became with time more conscious, accumulative, and systematic. But often it also suffered serious setbacks when people's attitudes, beliefs, and socio-political conditions all but stopped it. When Islam came on the scene of history this was the case. There was little interest in science and learning and whatever activity was going on in this direction was not even enough to preserve the fruits of earlier generations, much less to enable science to grow and realize its full potential. Europe, for example, had lost works even of its own men of learning and had plunged into its Dark Ages. The situation in other parts of the world was not much better.

Tremendous Islamic Impetus to Science

To such a dull and dying world of learning, Islam brought life and brilliance. As soon as Islam had finished the necessary task of establishing itself in the world and creating a suitable social order, there began to flourish under its shadow a most intense interest in science and learning.

Muslim rulers, many of whom were themselves scholars and writers, began to encourage and patronize all kinds of learning, such as the study and translation of the works of earlier civilizations, the synthesis of ideas and scientific observations from various sources, and new investigations. Princes and viziers vied with each other in establishing libraries and colleges.

Private citizens also used their own resources for learning and research. For example, Banu Musa, the three sons of Musa Ibn Shakir, "spent fabulous sums on the collection of manuscripts and the assembly of translations."[2] They also built a private observatory at home for their astronomical studies. There were, by the standards of those times, huge libraries. In the library of al-Aziz at Cairo, for example, there were more than 120,000 volumes, while that of al-Hakam at Cordova was even bigger. A minor college founded in Baghdad in 900 A.C. contained 10,400 books. As for individuals, "even in the first century of the Hegira we find learned men scolded by their wives for possessing great numbers of books and one was actually killed by the fall of a pile of folios which he had heaped around him while sitting on the floor."[3]

While some Muslim women scolded their husbands for their addiction to learning, others shared the addiction. Investigation discloses that women were lecturers as well as students. In Makka, Karima lectured on *Hadith* (prophetic tradition) and Shahida taught theology. Some of the most famed surgeons in Muslim Spain were women[4] and in literature "the names of Nashun, Zainab, Hamada, Hafsah, al-Kalayyeh, Safia, Maris, shed an ineffaceable lustre on the land of their birth."[5]

Muslim scholars also made tiresome journeys to collect information for their writings and researches. The saying attributed to the Prophet (SAWS): "Seek knowledge even if you have to go to China" is probably unauthentic, but it nevertheless speaks for the spirit of the time.

The significance of intense interest in science and learning among Muslims in the Middle Ages cannot be overestimated. It brought scientific activity to a level where its continued existence and growth and the realization of its fullest potential was ensured. In earlier times scientific activity used to flourish in some societies for a while and then fade away for lack of interest and suitable socio-political conditions. But the tremendous push it received from Islam gave it a momentum whereby it became a continuously present and global activity ever producing new results. Before Muslims themselves temporarily lost interest in science, they were able to transfer their enthusiasm for learning and the fruits of their labors to Europe, where science found an exceptionally fertile ground because it brought fresh air to societies suffocating under a narrow, superstitious, and dogmatic view of the world severely imposed by an authoritarian Church.

After the great development that it underwent in Europe, science has now begun to flourish again in the Muslim world and other parts of the East, and promises to attain a global presence that may be expected to last until the end of history. This would have been impossible without the impetus science received from the Muslims.

Influence on Christian Europe

It was in the later part of the Middle Ages, when science was still thriving in the Islamic world, the Muslim science began to interest and influence Europeans and created for the first time scientific activity in Christian Europe. We can trace almost every significant early development in Christian Europe in the direction of science and learning to Muslim influences. Europe's interest in its own men of learning was revived by Muslims. A leading Arabist says: "It can hardly be doubted that Europeans took up the study of Aristotle because their zeal for philosophy had been quickened by contact with Arabian thought. Indeed, if the first effective influence was not Arabian, how are we to explain the fact that for generations Aristotle was confounded with teaching ascribed to Averroes (Ibn Rushd)?"[6]

Much earlier, in 1291, Roger Bacon wrote: "The greater part of Aristotle's philosophy failed to have any effect (in the West) either because manuscripts were hidden away and extremely rare, or because the subject matter was difficult and distasteful, or because of the wars in the East, until after the time of Mahomet (Muhammad) when Avicenna (Ibn Sina) and Averroes (Ibn Rushd) and the rest brought back Aristotle's philosophy into the light of comprehensive exposition."[7]

All noteworthy European scientists and philosophers of the Middle Ages, such as Roger Bacon, Adelard of Bath, Leonard Fibonacci, Robert Crossette, and Peter of Maricourt, were either taught by Muslims or were dependent on Muslim works, because practically nothing was available in Europe on which any kind of study could be based. Emperor Frederick II, who had a keen interest - no doubt kindled by Muslim example - in mathematics, astronomy and philosophy, sent messengers to the Egyptian Sultan, Malik Kamil, with requests for answers to certain problems with which he was grappling. The Sultan obliged by sending some scholars to the emperor. Louis IX founded the first hospital in Paris after his return from the Crusades (1254-1260).[8] The establishment of other hospitals in Europe was also inspired by Muslim example. Later, colleges and universities were built under Muslim influence, being patterned at least in part on the Islamic institution of madrasah.[9]

Even Christian theology was indebted to Islamic philosophers. St. Thomas Aquinas, the outstanding Christian theologian of all times, "not only bears heavily on al-Farabi but (without direct acknowledgement) makes use of his most important concepts and arguments and, as often as not, quotes from him practically verbatim, especially from his *Gems of Wisdom* and *The Intellectual and the Intelligible Political Regime.*"[10]

The scientific learning that passed from Islam to Christian Europe in the Middle Ages contained much of the scientific achievements of earlier civilizations, enriched by the Muslims' own impressive contributions (see Appendix II). The Europeans did not have to go through the same painstaking process of collecting and sifting earlier works as the Muslims had to do. The material they found brought together by Muslims in a clear and comprehensive exposition not only later formed the basis for far-reaching scientific developments, but also contained suggestions in the direction of such developments. In particular, the most basic and efficient approach to science and learning characterizing "modern science" had already begun to crystalize in Muslim scientific works. We find Muslim scientists making very much the same kind of use of experiment, observation, mathematics, and theory-building that modern science considers its essential method and the source of its phenomenal development. Draper is among many scholars to have recognized this when he says:

The essential characteristics of their (i.e. the Muslims') method are experiment and observation. Geometrical and mathematical sciences they worked up as instruments of reasoning. In their numerous writings on mechanics, hydrostatics, optics, etc., it is interesting to remark that the solution to a problem is always obtained by performing an experimental observation. It was this that made them the originators of chemistry; that led them to the invention of all kinds of apparatus for distillation, sublimation, fusion, filtration, etc.; that caused them to appeal to divided instruments such as quadrants and astrolabes, in chemistry to employ the balance, the theory of which they were perfectly familiar with, to construct tables of specific gravity and astronomical tables like those of Baghdad and Spain, great improvements in geometry, the invention of algebra. Such were the results of the performance of the inductive method - their declining the reveries of Plato.[11] Here we may recall that Plato despised sense perception which, in his view, yielded mere opinion and no real knowledge.

Another historian puts the point more boldly:

What we call science arose in Europe as a result of a new spirit of inquiry, of new methods of investigation, of the method of experiment, observation, measurement of the development of mathematics in a form unknown to the Greeks. That spirit and those methods were introduced into the European world by the Arabs."[12]

Another characteristic of modern science is that it is directed not only towards satisfying man's urge for knowing the world around him but also toward solving practical problems man faces in his daily life. In this regard too, Muslim science appears to be of the same character as modern science. Bertrand Russell, who has written several books on the history of science and philosophy, rightly opens his *Science and Society* by tracing to the Arabs the origin of scientific activity as a systematic way of solving man's problems.

The Role of Islam

In many crucial ways Islam was directly responsible for the emergence of Muslim science and therefore of modern science. It was Islam that sent into the centers of the civilized world the unlettered Arabs whose freshness of mind enabled them to value the works of the earlier civilizations and look at them in a new way. Moreover, Islam sent the Arabs out with an unprecedented love and reverence for knowledge. It had already taught them that the greatest miracle of all time was a book - the Qur'an - and that the creation of man, despite his capacity for conflict and destruction, was justified in the sight of Allah because man could name things (2:30-33), meaning that he could think objectively about things. The Qur'anic revelation had started with the command:

Read in the name of Allah Who creates
Creates man from a blood-clot
Read: And thy Lord is the most bounteous

Who teaches man by the pen
Teaches him what he knew not.

> (Qur'an 96:1-5)

These verses show that *'il'm* (knowledge) is not always understood in the Qur'an in any restricted sense. In particular, it does not refer simply to the religious knowledge revealed through Prophet Muhammad (SAWS); for that knowledge, according to the Qur'an, did not come through the "pen".[13]

The possibility of man learning ever new things mentioned in this last verse is stated negatively in 17:85: "You have not received but a minute quantity of knowledge," and gives rise to the prayer in 20:114: "And say, O Lord! increase me in knowledge." Many sayings attributed to the Prophet also glorify knowledge and exhort men to acquire it.[14]

The degree of love and reverence for knowledge that these Islamic teachings inspired in some Muslims may be judged from a saying of one of the first disciples of Muhammad (SAWS). 'Ali ibn Talib is reported to have said: "Anyone who taught me a word, I became his slave."

But all this Muslim love and respect for knowledge would have come to almost nothing had it not been the case that Islamic teachings not only do not offend man's sense of reason but appeal to it. Again and again the Qur'an speaks to men who have understanding and who use *'AQL* (reason). Several times it confronts opponents with strong reasoning. Thus in 2:170 it gives in one sentence an argument that will ever point to the absurdity of slavery to tradition:

> When it is said to them, "Follow that which God has revealed," they say, "Nay, we shall follow the ways of our fathers." What! Even though their fathers were void of wisdom *(aql)* and guidance?" (2:170)

In 5:75-78 the Qur'an tries to bring trinitarian Christians in touch with the reality about the person of Jesus by the argument that he and his mother "both used to eat their daily bread (like the rest of mankind)."

Verses like 21:66 face the idol worshippers with reasoning: "Do ye worship besides Allah things that can neither do any good to you nor any harm?"

The oneness of Allah is supported by the logic that if two divine wills were operative in the universe there would be utter chaos in the universe (instead of the harmony and interrelatedness that we find). The disbelievers who ask, by way of an argument against resurrection, who will raise them to life after they become bones are told: "The same who created you the first time." I do not mean to say that every argument in the Qur'an will be convincing for everyone nor that everything in the Qur'an is logically supported. But the characteristic of logical reasoning that runs throughout the Qur'an enables faith not only to coexist with reason but to respect it and make use of it.

Islam was thus able to maintain over many centuries the love and respect for knowledge that it inspired among Muslims and enabled them to pursue learning without feeling any threat to the foundation on which their civilization came to be built.

In addition to reason the Qur'an also attaches great importance to the observation of natural phenomena. Again and again it draws men's attention to, or invites them to ponder upon, such phenomena as the motion of the heavenly bodies (36:37-40), the cycle of days and nights (17:12), the formation of clouds and rain (30:48), the earth's coming back to life with rain after its death (2:164), means of transport such as ships with all their potential for benefitting mankind (30:46, 31:31), the process of man's birth and his death (23:12-15), the separation between blood and milk in the body of a cow (16:66), the mountains and their role in adding stability to the earth (21:30-32; 31:10-11), the birds with their capacity to fly despite being heavier than air (67:19), and to man's own self and the knowledge ingrained in it (91:7-8). The Qur'an claims that its truth is manifested by what man can observe within himself and in the world without (41:53). It is natural then that the Qur'an affirms the seen world which is created "in truth" and "not in vain" (16:3; 3:191; 21:16-17).

A Muslim is instructed in Hadith not to close his eyes while praying because praying is not to close one's eyes to the world of perception, but to open oneself to the unseen world beyond. Islam's affirmation of the visible world around man and invitation to him to observe it must certainly have played a role in the development of the scientific method among Muslims.

If Islam contained material to encourage man to observe the world around him, its most fundamental doctrine, namely, the Oneness of Allah and the unity of His creation, provided an urge to unify and integrate observations and experiences. This urge is probably the most important single impulse behind scientific developments.

Islam also contributed to the development of science by creating the order and stability that was needed for the cultivation of learning. A concrete and illuminating example of this is provided by the following comments in a manuscript of al-Biruni written on the completion of certain geographical investigations, 21 September, 1025: [15]

Most of the data of the Geography (of Ptolemy) concerning the longitude and latitude of points on the earth have really been adopted only on the ground of rumors which had come from far-off districts. . . . Anyhow, the ground on which these data rest is mere report; indeed those lands were very difficult of access in the past owing to the national divisions *(At-tabayun Al-milli)*, for national division is the greatest obstacle to travel in countries. We see, for example, those who think - as do the Jews - to come nearer to God through treacherous attack on folk of other nationalities. Or they take foreigners as slaves, as do the Romans, and that is the lesser evil. Or travellers, because they are foreigners, are turned back, held in every kind of suspicion and they are thus brought to a very dangerous and unpleasant plight.

But now the circumstances are quite different. Islam has already penetrated from the eastern countries of the earth to the western; it spread westward to Spain (Andalus), eastward to the borderland of China and to the middle of India, southward to Abyssinia and the countries of Zanj (i.e. South Africa, the Malay Archipelago and Java), northward to the countries of the Turks and Slavs. Thus the different peoples *(al-umam al-mukhtalifah)* are brought together in mutual understanding *(ulfat)* which only God's own Act can bring to pass . . .

To obtain information concerning places of the earth has now become incomparably easier and safer (than it was before). Now we find a crowd of places, which in the (Ptolemaic) "Geography" are indicated as lying to the east of other places, actually situated to the west of the others named, and vice versa.

Islam was able to achieve a higher degree of order and stability and more favorable research conditions by inspiring that confident faith which is not easily threatened and which engenders magnanimity, by recognizing validity in all monotheistic faiths and teaching respect for them, by teaching tolerance and declaring that "there is no coercion in religion" (2:256), by preaching the universal brotherhood of man, and by giving a law that could organize societies on the basis of justice - the only basis on which durable and stable societies can be organized.

The Role of Christianity

In the New Testament and in the subsequent tradition built on it there is hardly anything that could cultivate learning in the wider sense in which we have been using the word. Indeed, being the work of several men from varied backgrounds, various parts of the Christian scriptures often conflict so violently with one another that a spirit of learning, which at the very least would demand consistency in contents, would be fatal for faith.

The spirit of learning, of course, would demand more than consistency. It would also examine the contents of the teachings and would discover that the most central of Christian teachings, e.g. the doctrines of trinity and redemption through the Cross, are not the kind of teachings that have roots in what man can know through his experience of the world both outside of himself and inside.[16] But it is precisely such experience on which the spirit of learning is based.

It is therefore no mere chance that for most of its two thousand years of history Christianity not only did not inspire a spirit of learning at an extensive level, but often suppressed it: Churchmen and crusaders were responsible for the destruction of hundreds of thousands of Greek and Muslim books[17] and for the persecution of scientists. Nor is it a coincidence that when science and learning did become widespread in Europe in spite of the Church, it was accompanied by a rejection or reduction of the authority of the Bible, and science became completely secularized.

But after the authority of the Bible was sufficiently restricted in Europe, and people could choose to reject the narrow interpretations of the Church, Christianity did play a positive role in the development of science. The teaching of love, on which emphasis increased as enlightenment increased, had created in Europe a spirit of constructiveness which found expression in the use of science and technology for improving the lot of man. This influence was enhanced further by the Christian belief that Jesus (AS) was or will be the bringer of the Kingdom of God, through which suffering and disease will be eliminated and the joy of man will be full.

Earlier Christians believed that Jesus (AS) partly realized the Kingdom of God through his church in a metaphysical way and that the full establishment of the Kingdom would take place at his Second Coming. With science and technology flourishing in Europe and the centers of learning well established and active in radically transforming European societies, Christian thought began to see in science and technology an instrument for realizing the Kingdom of God. In this way the Church gave to science and technology whatever moral support and spiritual power it could.

Christianity also strengthened the conception of an infinite and dynamic universe introduced in science by the Muslims. As Landau has noted, such a conception of the universe is connected with the belief in God. Commenting on Muslim science, Landau says:

> The Muslim ideal was, it goes without saying, not visual beauty but God in his plentitude; that is God with all His manifestations, the stars and the heavens, the earth and all nature. The Muslim ideal is thus infinite. But in dealing with the infinite as conceived by Muslims, we cannot limit ourselves to space alone, but must equally consider time.

The first mathematical step from the Greek concept of a static universe to the Islamic one of a dynamic universe was made by al-Khwarizmi (780-850), the founder of modern algebra. He enhanced the purely arithmetical character of numbers as finite magnitudes by demonstrating the possibilities as elements of infinite manipulations and investigations of properties and relations. In Greek mathematics numbers could expand only by the laborious process of addition and multiplication. Khwarizmi's algebraic symbols for numbers contain within themselves the potentialities of the infinite. So we might say that the advance from arithmetic to algebra implies a step from "being" to "becoming", from the static Greek universe to the living universe of Islam. The importance of Khwarizmi's algebra was recognized in the twelfth century by the West, when Gerard of Cremona translated his thesis into Latin. Until the sixteenth century this version was used in European universities as the principal mathematical text book. But Khwarizmi's influence reached far beyond the universities. We find it reflected in the mathematical works of Leonardo Fibonacci of Pisa, Master Jacob of Florence, and even of Leonardo da Vinci."[18]

For Muslims the universe is a living, changing manifestation of God's creativeness. The Qur'an says of Allah (SWT) "every day He is in a (new) glory" (55:29) and a saying of the Prophet (SAWS) advises us not to speak against time because Allah (SWT) is in a sense time (Al-Bukhari, 1 Adab, 101). A Muslim was the first person to speak of time as the fourth dimension.[19] Since Christianity too has something of the Islamic idea of God, it was able to support a dynamic, infinite idea of the universe as against the static, finite idea of the Greeks. Thus when controversy arose in Europe concerning infinite quantities, rejected by Aristotle, Christianity was prepared to recognize such quantities.[20]

Summarizing the above discussion, we can say that the act of Allah (SAWS) in the coming of Prophet Muhammad (SAWS) was directly responsible for the development of science as we know it today and for its global and perpetual existence and that in the last few centuries Christianity too has played a role, at least in putting science to a constructive use. In this way Islam, and to a lesser degree Christianity, have made a decisive contribution to the fulfillment of materialistic hopes, in as much as such hopes have been fulfilled through science.

NOTES

1. This is also shown by following tradition reported from Sa'd in Mishkat-al-Masabih. After praying for a long time to his Lord in a mosque of the children of Mu'awia, the Prophet said: "I asked my Lord for three things, of which He gave me two but refused one. I asked my Lord not to destroy my followers with famine and He granted it to me. I asked Him not to destroy my followers with flood and He granted it to me. But when I asked Him not to let war arise among themselves, He refused it to me." (XLIV/I/13; see also XLIV/I/15, where the second of the prayers granted is that no people may prevail over the Prophet's followers and uproot them.)

2. Gaston Wiet, et. al., *The Great Medieval Civilizations*, (London 1975), pp. 643-6.

3. Khuda Buksh, "The Educational Systems of the Muslims in the Middle Ages", *Islamic Culture*, July, 1927, p. 453.

4. S. H. Leeder, "The Debt of Civilization to the Arabs", *Islamic Review*, March 1916, p. 115.

5. Ameer Ali, *Short History of the Saracens*, p. 569.

6. A. Guillaume, quoted from Robert L. Gulick Jr., *Muhammad: The Educator*, Lahore, p. 75.

7. Quoted from Gulick, op.cit., p. 75.

8. Rom Landau, *Islam and the Arabs,* London, 1958, p. 180.

9. Khalil I. Semaan, Ed. *Islam and the Medieval West* (State University of New York Press, Albany, 1980.

10. Rom Landau, op.cit., p. 147.

11. William Draper, *Conflict Between Science and Religion.*

12. Robert Briffault, *The Making of Humanity,* pp. 190-191.

13. See also note 14 below.

14. See Robert L. Gulick, op.cit., pp. 45-48. Some of the sayings of the Prophet (SAWS) seem to refer to religious knowledge specifically, as, for example, this tradition from al-Bukhari: "The learned are the heirs of the prophets who have transmitted to them knowledge as a legacy. He who has chosen learning has taken a great portion and for him who engages himself in the way of acquiring knowledge, Allah will pave the path to the very gates of Paradise." But in other prophetic traditions the reference is to knowledge more generally, as in the following tradition, again from al-Bukhari: "There are only two persons whom one is permitted to envy: the one to whom Allah has given riches and who has the courage to spend his means for the cause of truth; the other to whom Allah has given wisdom and who applies it for the benefit of mankind and shares it with his fellows."

15. Ahmad Zeki Validi, "Islam and the Science of Geography", *Islamic Culture,* October, 1934, pp. 417-8.

16. These doctrines, in fact, originated from historical necessity rather than from any genuine experience, prophetic or otherwise. The doctrine of trinity, which was finally decided upon by a show of hands (not unanimously) in the Council of Nicea in 325 A. C., merely reflects the historical fact that on the one hand the glorification of Jesus and the Holy Spirit had reached a point where many believers could no longer think of anyone of these two beings as second to God, and where, on the other hand, the Oneness of God had such strong roots in the Bible and the earlier Christian tradition that they could not be cut off. The dogma of redemption through the Cross is a solution, inspired by the mythologies of the time, to the problem caused by the fact that Jesus' first coming did not realize the expected Kingdom of God and his second coming did not materialize within the lifetime of his contemporaries as expected. To a certain extent every dogma or doctrine is connected with certain historical circumstances. While some doctrines (such as the central Islamic doctrine of the Oneness of God and the accountability of man) have a meaning and validity apart from the historical circumstances in which they were realized and were in fact discovered by people in various times and places and under various historical circumstances, the central Christian doctrines were entirely the creation of some historical situations and were never independently generated from any other historical situation.

17. For example, in 389 A.C., the celebrated library of Serapis at Alexandria was ruined on the order of Archbishop Theophilus. According to Gustav Dierecks ("Europe's Debt to Islam", *Islamic Review,* May, 1928, p. 138) the guiding principle of Pope Gregory was; "Ignorance is the mother of piety." Acting on this principle, Gregory burned the precious Palatine library founded by Emperor Augustus, destroyed the greater part of the writings of Livy and forbade the study of the classics. The

Crusaders destroyed the splendid library of Tripoli and reduced to ashes many of the glorious centers of Saracenic art and culture (see Ameer Ali, op.cit., p. 351). Ferdinand and Isabella put to flames all the Muslim works they could find in Spain.

18. Rom Landau, *Islam and the Arabs*, London, 1958, p. 168-169.

19. S. H. Nasr, *Islamic Science* (London, 1976), p. 139.

20. Gaston Wiet, op.cit., p. 667.

Chapter VI

Fulfillment of Nationalistic Hopes

The wonderful, universalistic hopes discussed in the last two chapters and fulfilled in a remarkable way through the work of the "messianic trinity" present us with only one side of the picture. Side by side with these hopes we find in the Old Testament purely nationalistic and even racist hopes. If some parts of the Old Testament hope for the house of God in Jerusalem to become a house of prayer for all nations, the following passage from the Book of Ezekiel would allow none but the children of Israel to enter it:

> Thus saith the Lord God, foreigners (being) uncircumcised in heart and flesh, shall not enter my sanctuary, not even those foreigners who live among the children of Israel. (Ezek. 44:9)

While some parts of the Old Testament picture the messianic future in terms of a brotherhood of man founded on the worship of the one and only God, the following verse pictures humanity as divided into nations or races, each worshipping its own god:

> For all people will walk everyone in the name of his god and we will walk in the name of Yahweh our god for ever and ever. (Micah 4:5)

And in contrast to the passages that hope for the whole of humanity to share the materialistic benefits of messianic times, only desolation is hoped for some nations in the following passage:

> And it shall come to pass in that day that the mountains shall drop down new wine, and the hills shall flow with milk, and all the rivers of Judah shall flow with water . . . Egypt shall be a desolation, and Eden shall be a desolate wilderness . . . but Judah shall dwell for ever. (Joel 3:18-20)

The tribal deity, Yahweh, and the Jewish nationalism connected with it are seen naked in passages such as those quoted above. In many other passages, however, this idolatrous nationalism is ambiguously fused with higher universalist conceptions of Allah, so that one is left wondering whether it is the universal God who is using the nation of Israel to exalt and reveal Himself or whether it is the nation of Israel that is using the universal God to exalt itself.

These two ambiguously fused meanings or intentions behind the messianic prophecy gradually begin to get separated and find expression in distinct developments in subsequent history. On the one hand, we see the messianic prophecy inspiring the universal religion of Christianity that was later perfected by the Islamic revelation of a *truly* universal God, Allah (see Chap. IV), a revelation that broke down all kinds of barriers between nations and races and *at the same time brought for the Jews their Golden Age.*[1] On the other hand, we see the Jews sticking to the national idol, perpetuating barriers between themselves and other peoples and waiting or struggling for political and religious supremacy over the rest of mankind, *but succeeding only in bringing disaster and humiliation on themselves.*

We see in the first two centuries B.C. the Essenes separating themselves from the rest of the world into isolated "messianic" communities by the Dead Sea and waiting for God to fight and destroy all the nations and the "wicked" among their own fellow Jews. A little later the Zealots wage an armed struggle to restore the Davidic kingdom with its rule extended over the whole world. The well-known result of such messianic movements was the destruction of the Temple and the dispersion of the Jews among the very nations they sometimes wished to see annihilated. The challenge of life in the diaspora only increased the communal spirit, so they held on to the idol of the nation all the more tenaciously.

Jews often isolated themselves in ghetto-like communities, leading what was basically a self-centered, cultish, and communal existence, in which they looked upon the host nations as nothing more than markets to be exploited. The results of these attitudes, especially when they provoked Christian prejudices, were persecutions and gas chambers. In better times, these attitudes produced the State of Israel. It is an indication of the type of spirit that the Jews have kept alive over the ages that, even after living outside of Palestine for two thousand years, they could claim that country to be theirs and wage war to regain it.

This history of the Jews becomes comprehensible only when we realize that even though the Jewish mind had conceived a transcendent, universal God, the Jewish heart never really abandoned the tribal and territorial idol that Yahweh often was. The battlefield of modern Palestine, the gas chambers of Auschwitz, and the ghettos of medieval Europe can be understood only as fruits of devotion to this idol, that is, as an ongoing historical representation of the particular interpretation of the messianic prophecy which exalts in Israel. If the result of this self-exaltation has generally been suffering and humiliation for the Jews, it is only because, as Jesus said, "He who exalts himself shall be humbled" (Luke 14:11).

The State of Israel

Let us now come to a more detailed consideration of the nationalistic hopes from the point of view of their fulfillment or otherwise. Throughout history there have been numerous attempts by the Jews to fulfill these hopes, but of these only the modern state of Israel has not yet proved to be a complete failure. We shall therefore concentrate our attention on this Jewish effort. Later, however, we shall also consider the Islamic and Christian approaches to the Jewish nationalistic hopes.

The starting point for the creation of the state of Israel, as a conscious attempt by the Jewish people to fulfill the messianic prophecies, is clearly provided by the Old Testament promise that one day all the Jews will gather in Palestine from all parts of the world, practice their religion wholeheartedly and form a prosperous kingdom ruled by the descendents of David. Such promises are scattered throughout the Old Testament and we have encountered them in earlier chapters. We may nevertheless quote as samples the following two passages from the Book of Ezekiel, to state the matter once again in the language of the Old Testament itself:

> I will even gather you from the people, and assemble you out of the countries where ye have been scattered, and I will give you the land of Israel. And they shall come thither, and they shall take away all the detestable things thereof and all the abominations thereof from thence. And I will give them one heart, and I will put a new spirit within you; and I will take the stony heart out of their flesh, and will give them an heart of flesh that they may walk in my statutes, and keep mine ordinances, and do them. . . .
>
> (Ezek 11:17-20)

> For thus saith the Lord God; Behold, I will search my sheep (i.e. Children of Israel) and seek them out . . . And I will bring them

out from the people, and gather them from the countries, and will
bring them to their own land, and feed them upon the mountains
of Israel by the rivers . . . I will feed my flock and I will cause them
to lie down (in comfort), saith the Lord . . . And I will set up one
shepherd over them, my servant, Daivd (i.e. descendants of David)
and he shall feed them. . . .

(Ezek. 34:11-23)

From a historical point of view nothing is more understandable than
the concern for the land of Israel shown in these and other similar passages. The Hebrews originally were semi-nomadic people who managed
to get a land in the time of Joshua and form some kind of nation but
who, due to the unique position of their land on the map of the world,
were often caught in the middle of conflicts between great empires in
the neighborhood. They found it unusually difficult to prosper as a nation
and sometimes even to stay in the land. For people of such fortune it
was entirely natural that they should prize a settled existence on their
land more than is usual.

Furthermore, there was the idea found in earlier parts of the Old Testament but abandoned in the later, that Yahweh's sovereignty was restricted
to one particular land,[2] the land of Canaan, which also goes some way
in explaining the Jews' peculiar attachment to what is supposedly their
land. Understandable though this attachment may be, however, it cannot be said that its continuation into modern times has any valid religious basis. The fact that parts of the Old Testament promise to the Jews
the land of Palestine and restrict Yahweh's sovereignty to it does not provide such a basis. The Old Testament concerns itself with many things
that the Jews today do not or cannot accept. For example, many of the
Old Testament laws such as stoning for adultery or blasphemy have no
place in modern Jewish life. Again, the prophecy that the messianic kingdom will be ruled by Davidic kings is an example of an Old Testament
idea that can no longer have any validity since no one can now trace
his descent to David. The presence of other false and contradictory
prophecies in the Old Testament to which we drew attention in Chapter
II also shows that the Jews cannot regard themselves bound by every
prophecy in their Scriptures. It is the religious insight gained from those
scriptures as a whole and from other agencies for man's education and
spiritual enrichment that we must use to answer our question whether
the Jews' continued concern for a particular land is religiously justified
or not.

The Jews' own history has shown that the God revealed in the Old

Testament can be worshipped and obeyed outside of the land of Palestine. Most of the Jews for most of their long history have lived outside of that land and worshiped God and tried to live by His commandments as they understood them. In principle there is thus no absolute religious necessity that the Jews live in Palestine if they are to be acceptable to God.

It may seem attractive, however, to argue that the Jews need a land of their own to practice some injunctions of their law that cannot be otherwise easily obeyed or obeyed at all.[3] But on closer examination the argument loses all its attraction. For one thing, it is doubtful whether the end of true religion or even the Old Testament religion is perfect adherence to a prescribed code of law. Moreover, while in theory it may seem possible to institute a religious code of law if people accepting that code have a state of their own, in practice nothing created more disrespect and disobedience for that code than such a state. This we can see in the case of the State of Israel itself. The Jews there have far less love and respect for their traditions than those in the Diaspora and incline towards secularism. Many writers[4] justify the creation of the State of Israel on the grounds that such a state is needed to enable the Jews to practice their religion to perfection. But these same writers are forced to lament that many Israelis do not like to think of themselves as Jews, but simply as citizens of a state in secular terms, and that many do not care for the Jewish code of law.

In the Old Testament, nationalistic hopes can perhaps be justified on the grounds that the Jewish people needed a country to develop certain religious systems, preserve the conception of one transcendent God, and protect themselves from heathen practices and idolatry. But such a justification no longer exists: the basis for Jewish religion - the Old Testament - was completed more than two thousand years ago; idolatry and other heathen practices were abandoned by the Palestinians and inhabitants of other neighboring countries after the advent of Islam in the seventh century; instead these countries have adopted monotheism and many of the principles and practices of the Old Testament religion.

It is difficult to think of any religious purpose in the Old Testament that has now been served by the creation of the State of Israel. Perhaps one or two of its prophecies have been partially fulfilled through that event, but in doing so it has also violated the principles of peace and justice, with which Old Testament prophecy concerns itself almost as much as it does with the ingathering of the tribes in the land of Palestine. The State of Israel was created by the manifestly unjust action of displacing people who had lived in Palestine for more centures[5] than the Jews themselves had: it has become the single biggest danger to international peace. The State of Israel was the ultimate cause of disruption in the oil market in the seventies which, in turn, was the main cause of much economic instability in the world during that time. Moreover, the conflict between the Israelis and the Palestinians has involved the whole world and has therefore the potential of throwing the entire globe into the flames of war.

For the Jews, too, the State of Israel has done nothing good except to provide temporary satisfaction for a perverse attachment to a piece of land and a long dead past. The support that the Christian West was willing to give to the Jews following the Nazi atrocities in the Second World War is becoming less and less wholehearted because Western interests no longer coincide with those of the State of Israel. If the Jews go too far in manipulating the West, as they must if Israel is to survive, a serious type of anti-semitism may return. More that that, the Zealot-type selfdestructive Jewish extremism, always held in check in the diaspora, has begun to germinate[6] again in the land of Israel. The results for the Jews may be as disastrous as those of the Zealot movement in the first century A.D., as well as the rebellious nationalism of the sixth century B.C., which led to the Exile and the destruction of the Temple by the Babylonians.[7] Many Jews try to reconcile their emotional nationalism with their deeper, spiritual instincts by considering their nationalistic and Zionist pursuits, specifically the secular creation of the State of Israel, as a first step towards higher universal religious goals: a perfect Jewish state in Palestine will shine as an example of godliness that will be emulated by the whole of mankind. Increasingly, however, religious Jews are casting doubts on the capacity of states to be perfect and to provide religious enlightenment. Some now ask how many thousands of years must mankind wait for the first step toward their enlightenment to be completed? So far the Jewish nationalistic and Zionist concerns have set the example only for self-destructive extremism or arbitrary, unjust and belligerent claims to geographical and political expansion without limit on others' land. The fact is that Jews have made their best contribution to the enlightment of mankind not as citizens of a Jewish state in Palestine, but as people dispersed in other lands. And more than that, Christianity and Islam have shown, by example, that the best of the Jewish tradition can spread throughout the world by spiritual and intellectual leadership, not by the forced establishment of secular power.

We conclude, in the light of the above discussion, that from a religious point of view the creation of the State of Israel is as pointless as any earlier Jewish effort to fulfill the nationalistic hopes. It is just another offering in human flesh and blood to the national and territorial idol, and it is just as futile as any other expression of devotion to an idol.

Christianity, Islam, and Nationalistic Hopes

In its earliest stages of development, Christianity was sympathetic to Jewish nationalistic, messianic hopes. An early saying from Q (Luke 22:29), Matt. 19:28), possibly going back to Jesus himself,[8] promises that the Jews will have a kingdom in which the twelve disciples will govern the twelve tribes of Israel, and Jesus himself will presumably be the King of the nation as a whole. This prophecy of course was not fulfilled and, at least in the form in which it is found in Luke and Matthew, the promise is not meant to be fulfilled in history. Since it does not take into account the historical fact the Christianity had become an entirely gentile religion by the middle of the second century, this saying is not relevant even to the state of affairs in the last days, the Age beyond history. When, according to Christian belief, Jesus will return toward the end of history on clouds of heaven, he will do so as King and Saviour of the Christians (almost all gentile) and destroy the non-Christians (Luke 19:27; 2 Thess. 1:8; Rev. 2:25-27, 19:15). This paints a picture of the last days to which a Jewish kingdom, with Jesus as its King and the disciples as his governors for the twelve Jewish tribes, would hardly seem to be relevant.

Thus, apart from sharing for a brief period some national messianic hopes which it could not fulfill, Christianity, as understood in the light of the New Testament as a whole, ignores these nationalistic hopes and, in any case, does not expect them to be fulfilled in history. Furthermore, at least Jesus himself would have opposed any artificial or forced efforts to bring about the fulfillment of messianic prophecies (Matt. 11:12-13; Luke 16:16), the kind of efforts that in our times have gone into the creation of the State of Israel.

Islam is more consistent and categorical in rejecting the Jewish type of nationalism and the messianic hopes connected with it. The Qur'an nowhere affirms any of the nationalistic hopes in the Old Testament. It firmly denies, as we have already seen in Chapter IV, that revelation or salvation or victory in any way belongs exclusively or finally to the Jews or to any group formed by, or around, them.

The Qur'an regards the destruction of the Jewish country, once by the

Babylonians and then by the Romans, as divine punishment for the Jews' arrogance and rebelliousness (17:3-7) and then goes on to say:

> Maybe (O Children of Israel!) your Lord will yet have mercy on you. But if you return (to these ways), then We shall also return (to punishment) (17:8).

This suggests strongly that any attempt on the part of the Jews to return to the politics that led to the two earlier destructions will once again lead to a similar disaster. In particular, the State of Israel, founded as it is on injustice, on disregard for international law, and on a total disregard for the fundamental teachings of all the world's major religions, including Judaism, is probably doomed to destruction. Some prophetic traditions also point in the same direction.[9]

But the Islamic rejection of Jewish nationalism and messianic hopes connected with it does not originate from any hostility towards the Jewish people, such as we find in the New Testament.[10] Islam respectfully accepts many of the universalist religious principles of the Old Testament, makes Jerusalem a holy place (17:1), and leaves the door of God's mercy and salvation open to the Jews (17:8) even while they are outside the fold of Islam (5:72). Islam rejects Jewish nationalism because Islam intends to build the foundations for a universal brotherhood of man and such a brotherhood cannot be built on principles that incorporate anything of the Old Testament idea of a race eternally set apart, over and above the rest of mankind. For this same reason, Islam arose outside of the Jewish nation. For if Islam had originated from among the Jews the idea would have continued that revelation and salvation belong to the "chosen" people of Israel. The national idol of the Israelites could not have been effectively broken,[11] which is precisely what had to be done to build the basis for a universal brotherhood. We may note, incidentally, that by arising from among the Arabs and not the Jews, Islam does not violate all the Old Testament expectations.[12]

One of the greatest beneficiaries of Islamic universalism was, ironically, the Jews themselves. It is a fact of history recognized even by Jewish historians that Islam came as a great mercy to Judaism and the Jewish people. Dimont calls the medieval period of Jewish history under Islam the golden age for the Jews, and Goitein remarks: "Never has Judaism encountered such a close and fructitious symbiosis as that with the medieval civilization of Arab Islam."[13] Thus, while religious nationalism had several times brought destruction upon the Jews, Islam by rejecting that type of nationalism created a world order in which Jews could prosper as never before.

This was in the past, but even in the future many of the hopes of the Jews as a people can be naturally fulfilled through Islam once they stop trying to fulfill them exclusively through their own efforts rather than by reliance on God. Messianic hopes, as Jesus said, are not fulfilled by conscious human struggle but naturally like the growing of a seed by itself (Mark 4:26-29). This is clearly seen in the Islamic fulfillment of universalist, messianic hopes. There are very rare references in the Islamic sources to specific messianic prophecies; we can say with certainty that it was not a conscious plan of Prophet Muhammad (SAWS) and his successors to bring about the fulfillment of these prophecies. And yet Islam was able to fulfill within the lifetime of the Prophet's companions (RS) many messianic predictions; it was, for example, able to introduce the worship of the God of Abraham and Jacob to the Egyptians, Assyrians and other nations (Isa. 19:18-25) and to rebuild the destroyed temple of Solomon as a "house of prayer for all nations" (Isa. 56:7).

For the national aspirations of the Jews to find surer and more permanent fulfillment than provided by the State of Israel, it is essential that the Jews stop trying to exalt themselves. Their national narcissism must be healed. This is possible if they accept Islam; for at this stage in history their acceptance of a prophet not from among them can only be a cause and a sign of the healing of the effects of their excessive and centuries-old preoccupation with themselves. In Islam they would not lose their national identity, for no nation or group has ever lost its identity because of Islam; rather they would lose only a certain attitude toward their nation. The result would be a genuine fulfillment of many of their national aspirations expressed in the Old Testament. They will, for example, naturally occupy a prestigious position among mankind because of their past contribution to the development of many religious principles and institutions, just as the Arabs occupy a certain prestigious position in the Muslim world because of the fact that they were the first bearers of Islamic revelation (although nothing in Islam guarantees them such a position).

In this way, the prophecy of Zephaniah about the Jews will be fulfilled: "I will turn their shame to honor, and all the world will praise them." (3:19). They will be able to move in and out of Palestine as they please, without having to have a State and to wage wars to maintain it, although it is unlikely that many of them would want to live in that country. Palestine will become one of the major centers of religious learning and instruction, thus fulfilling the prophecy "that the law of God shall go forth from Zion" (Isa. 2:3). And, of course, the Jews and Palestine will share an increased material prosperity, which would follow a more peaceful brotherhood of man in Islam. It seems thus that even the key to a genuine fulfillment of nationalistic hopes is held by Islam, with its proclamation of the brotherhood of man and exaltation of the one true God, Allah (SWT).

NOTES

1. Max I. Dimont, *Jews, God, and History*, Signet Books, 1962, pp. 184-205.

2. See Note 3, Chp. I.

3. See Eliezer Berkovits, "Identity Problems in the State of Israel", *Judaism*, Vol. 28, No. 3, 1979, 334-44.

4. Eliezer Berkovits, op.cit.

5. It is not certain when the Jews as a well defined people can be said to"own" the land of Palestine, but it must certainly be quite some time after Moses (around 1500B.C.). Since the Jews left Palestine in the first century A. C. this meant that Jews have been in that land for less than fifteen centuries. In contrast, the people we now call Palestinians must be considered as possessing Palestine for most of the last twenty centuries.

6. In the face of opposition from outside and inside Israel, the zeal of those Israelis who want to extend the borders of Israel as they see them defined in the Old Testament - and these borders will include the whole of Jordon - is increasing. And along with the secularism of some Israelis, the religious bigotry of others is also on the increase.

7. See Chap. IV. J. Allegro, *The Chosen People*, Panther Books, 1973, despite making some drastic assumptions about the origin and nature of Judaism, has correctly brought out the exclusivist and racist trait in the Jewish heart, that led to the destruction of the Temple in 70 A.C. and the tragic suicide at Masada by the remnant Zealots when all their political - messianic hopes were shattered. But it should be repeated here that there was in Judaism a more positive trait to which Allegro fails to do justice and which found full development in Islam (see Chap IV.).

8. See A. Shafaat, *Jesus and the Messianic Figures*, unpublished, Chap. IV.

9. A. A. Maudoodi, *Khatm-e-nabuwwat* (Urdu), Lahore, 1963, pp. 64-67.

10. Despite the fact that the New Testament retains something of the religious nationalism of the Old Testament in that it sees salvation as somehow coming from the seed of Israel, the New Testament can be very hostile to the Jews and their leaders when it is concerned with their rejection of Jesus and Christianity. The Gospels are full of bitter attack on Jewish scribes; they attempt to put all the blame for Jesus' execution on the Jews, and the Gospel of John even calls them Children of the Devil (8:44).

11. Christianity does not disprove this point, but proves it. As we saw earlier, Christianity could not effectively break the idol of nationalism and racism (see Chap. IV). The attitude of the New Testament toward the Old Testament view of the people of Israel is basically one of approval, so that the two Testaments cannot fail to put nationalistic suggestions in the hearts of their readers. The nationalism of European countries in the past few centuries was the result of a transference by various European nations to themselves of the dreams for power and glory that parts of the Old Testament see for the Israelites. In a sense nationalism and racism of Nazi Germany and some of the other European countries was almost as Biblical as the State of Israel.

12. The Book of Genesis promises Abraham that mankind will be blessed through his descendents (Gen. 12:1-3). According to both the Qur'an and the Bible the Arabs descend from Abraham via his first-born son Ishmael. Later parts of Genesis exclude the Ishmaelites from this promise and restrict it to the descendents of Isaac and Jacob (Gen. 25:23,24; 28:13-16), although no reason is given for this exclusion. If anything, it is Isaac and Jacob who appear in Genesis as less than deserving to be a source of blessing for the whole of mankind, for they are seen acquiring the inheritance of their fathers through means not entirely legal and just. In the books of the prophets, whatever blessing is foreseen for mankind also comes through the example and medium of the children of Israel (=Jacob), but at least one prophet, Second Isaiah, is not averse to God using a non-Israelite as a main agent for His purpose. He sees in the Persian emperor Cyrus such an agent and actually calls him the Messiah of God (44:28, 45:1). When many of his people spoke ill of him and even complained against Yahweh for handing over the task of reestablishing Zion to a king who was not from Israel, he was inspired to say:

> Shall the clay say to him that fashioneth it, What makest thou? or thy work say, He hath no hands (skill)?

> Woe unto him that saith unto his father, What begettest thou? to the woman, What hast thou brought forth? Thus saith the Lord, . . . I have raised him (i.e. Cyrus) up in righteousness, and I will direct all his ways: he shall build my city, and he shall let go my captives . . ."
>
> (45:9-13)

In addition to Cyrus another Gentile emperor was also viewed as the Messiah by the Jews in his time. There is evidence that the Jewish contemporaries of Alexander the Great, dazzled by his glorious achievements, hailed him as the divinely appointed deliverer, the inaugurator of the time of universal peace and prosperity promised by the prophets, a view that later gave rise to some legends about the Greek conqueror. (The Jewish Encyclopedia, Vol. 8, p. 507)

13. S. D. Goitein, *Jews and Arabs - Their Contact Through the Ages*, New York, 1955, p. 130.

Conclusion

Let us summarize the main conclusion of our study:

1.   In the Old Testament the conception of God varies from that of a national god to that of the one true God, the Creator and Lord of the whole universe. The nationalistic conception of God can sink so low as to conceive Yahweh as literally the god of the Israelites, who exists along with the gods of other nations and who even has a territory (Canaan) to which his sovereignty is confined, so much so that to move out of that territory is to move "away from Yahweh" (I Sam. 26:19-20). Before the Old Testament was completed, Jewish thought returned to the original revelation through Abraham and Moses of a universal and monotheistic idea of God, but the Jewish heart always kept its devotion to the older national and territorial deity.

2.   Corresponding to the two conceptions of God there are to be found two types of messianic prophecies: those that limit salvation to the Israelites or a remnant of them, and those that extend it more universally. But even in the universalist, messianic hopes, the idea of the supremacy of the Israelites is not abandoned and the religious principles enshrined in them do not become truly universal. Only in the post-Old-Testament history of Semitic religion do we find the universal element developing toward complete transcendence over the national. In two stages, through Christian and Islamic revelation, the conception of God and His judgement and salvation achieved a complete break with the nationalistic limitations imposed on it throughout the incomplete remains of the original revelation in the Old Testament. In this way Islam (with Christianity playing a preparatory role) restored the purity of divine revelation and carried it to completion.

3.   Messianic prophecies should not be viewed only as providing detailed descriptions of future events that must necessarily come to pass;

in fact, as predictions of the future, messianic prophecies are untrust-
worthy, since they include demonstrably false and manifestly contradictory predictions. Nor was prediction the primary concern of the prophets
who wrote or uttered the messianic prophecies. Their concern rather
was either to make certain revelations about God and His moral demands
and judgements or to tell their contemporaries what ought to be the state
of affairs in their country and thus to inspire them toward a certain
course of action.

4.   Christianity and Islam fulfill the messianic prophecies in a double
sense. Firstly, as we noted above, they carried in two stages the revelatory principles enshrined in those prophecies to full development.
Secondly, they have inspired in history certain developments that have
an impressive correspondence to the picture of the future found in the
universalist, messianic prophecies. In this way the soundness of the logic
and profoundness of the religious insight that inspired those prophecies
is supported but not necessarily the ability to predict on the part of the
prophets who produced them.

5.   The best case for Christian fulfillment of the universalist, messianic
predictions is briefly presented in the following words of H. H. Rowley
in *From Moses to Qumran*, Lutterworth Press, London, 1963, pp. 26-27:

> The Old Testament declared that Israel was called to be the light
> of the nations and that her law was destined for all men and her
> God was to be worshipped by all. It also recognized that not all who
> were of the nation of Israel were worthy of their election, but
> declared that a remnant would inherit the privilege and the task
> that were hers, to be joined by proselytes from the Gentiles who
> would then share her election and her mission. Those remarkable
> prophecies have been fulfilled in the Christian Church to a degree
> that is surely impressive. The Church was founded by a company
> of Jews, a Remnant of Israel, who accepted the mission of Israel
> to the world seriously . . . Today the Hebrew Scriptures are trans-
> lated into countless tongues and cherished by millions of people
> who would never have heard of them through the Jews alone, and
> Israel's God is worshipped in almost every land under heaven.

Christian scholars do not do justice to the history of religion beyond
Christianity, despite the fact that a global religious development of
tremendous scope, namely, Islam, emerged in history after Jesus and
outside of the Christian church. If one gives due consideration to the
phenomenon of Islam, one can see clearly that through Islam the reali-

zation of the messianic hopes reaches a final stage. Thus, although Christianity carried something of the Jewish idea of God "in almost every land under heaven," it did so only after corrupting it with redemptive and trinitarian myths that are completely antagonistic to the original spirit of semitic revelation, whether through Moses, Jesus or Muhammad (AS). In contrast to this, Islam took to every land the worship of a God Whom one can still find revealed in parts of the Old Testament despite later accretions by those with less understanding.

Similarly, while it is true that through the Church the Hebrew Scriptures are today "translated into countless tongues and cherished by millions of people," the Church has done so only after declaring everything in the Jewish holy book out of date, except what it considers to be predictions about Jesus. In contrast, Islam established in the world a developed and integrated form of many of the doctrines, practices, and laws found in the Jewish scriptures, such as respectively, monotheism, circumcision, and abstinence from pork, etc. Indeed, the affinity between Judaism and Islam is often noted. Moreover, Islam also made possible the fulfillment of the materialistic, messianic hopes by inspiring the development of modern science, while Christianity played no direct role in improving the material lot of man, at least not until long after the advent of Islam.

6. The view that Islam (with Christianity playing a preparatory role) fulfills the messianic prophecies is rooted in the teachings of the Prophets Jesus and Muhammad (AS) themselves. Jesus taught that the fulfillment of messianic prophecies started with the advent of John the Baptist, continued in his own work, and would be consummated with the universal manifestation of Man or son of Man. A similar view must be held on the basis of the Qur'an, which teaches, moreover, that the universal manifestation of Man expected by Jesus and others before him took place in the coming of the Prophet Muhammad (SAWS). This means that fulfillment of messianic prophecies took place through the work of the three messengers of God, John the Baptist, Jesus Christ and the Prophet Muhammad (AS), i.e. through Christianity and Islam.

7. Finally, the self-exaltation of Judaism in a secular Israel is one of the major tragedies in history. While Christianity and Islam completed the universalist element in the Old Testament religion and fulfilled its universalist hopes, the Jews themselves held on, at least in practice, to a nationalistic religion with racist and Zionist ambitions. They took their lonely journey through history, trying to establish a Jewish kingdom or state or prove their superiority in other ways. In such efforts they occasionally achieved partial and temporary successes, but their self-

exaltation always returned them to a state of misery in contrast to their dreams of glory and power. The modern State of Israel is one of the Jews' brief success stories, but this must be the last. The tribal deity of Canaan is no longer up against the idols of the heathen as in the past, but against the one true God, Allah, the Creator and Lord of the whole universe, who has spoken through all the prophets since the beginning of mankind, to warn that all idols, and all who worship such false gods, are sure to be destroyed.

Suffering and the Messianic Figures

T he numerous passages in the Old Testament that contain the theme of suffering do not treat this theme in connection with the Messiah or with the coming of the messianic age. In pre-Christian times, Judaism never made such a connection. (See Joseph Klausner, *The Messianic Idea in Israel,* tr. W. F. Stinespring, London, 1956, p. 405-407, 483-501). Nevertheless the peculiar circumstances in which Christian faith in the Messiahship of Jesus arose has made many passages about suffering important in Christian literature and some discussion of the theme seems appropriate here.

Probably the Christians' favorite passage in which they see the vicarious suffering of Jesus foretold is the Fourth Servant Song (ISA. 52.13 - 53.12). The song opens with an introductory passage which briefly advances the theme of the future exaltation of someone called Yahweh's servant after his suffering and rejection. In the following translation the King James Version has been modified in accordance with the generally accepted conclusions of critical research into the original Hebrew text.

Behold, my servant will prosper
He will be exalted and extolled and be very high.
As many were astonished at thee - So his appearance was marred more than any man
and his form more than sons of men.
So will he startle many nations
The Kings shall shut their mouths at him
for that which had not been told shall they see
and that which they had not heard shall they consider.

The identity of the person referred to as the servant of Yahweh was hotly disputed by past generations of Biblical scholars. But today most scholars agree that the Servant is not a future person but a past or present figure and that he is either a righteous remnant of the Israelites, personified by an individual, or an actual individual such as the Second Isaiah or some other prophet. If the servant is some historical prophetic figure, then what did he suffer? The song does not give us a certain answer. Reference to his appearance being disfigured (52:14), as one despised, from whom people hid their faces (53:3) and considered stricken by God (53:4), bruised and put to grief by God (53:10), suggests a person suffering from a disease like leprosy. On the other hand, verses like 53:7-9 present a picture of a person persecuted and enduring extremely harsh treatment by society.

It is also not clear how the suffering of the servant, if he is an individual prophet, ended. The statements in 53:8-9 that the servant "was cut off from the land of the living" or that "with the wicked his grave was assigned, and with the rich in his deaths (or sepulchral mounds)" do not necessarily imply that death ended the servant's suffering. In ancient Israelite thought, illness and misfortune could be considered akin to death, without implying the actual occurrence of death: "Those who are suffering, or those who have been healed, speak of their illness (or of other menacing deadly dangers) as a descent into Sheol, a sojourn in the grave, a real death. From this state of death they pray to God to deliver them; or they thank Him because He has done so . . ." (S. Mowinckel, *He That Cometh*, pp. 234-35).

The exaltation and restoration of the servant is described in less ambiguous terms than the nature and conclusion of his sufferings. In the introductory passage we are told that the servant will prosper and amaze nations and kings. The concluding passage speaks in more detail:

> He will see his seed, he will prolong his days
> and the pleasure of Yahweh shall prosper in his hand.
> He shall see of the (result of) the travail of his soul,
> and shall be satisfied;
> By his knowledge shall my righteous servant justify many and he
> shall bear their iniquities.
> Therefore will I give him a portion among the great, and he shall
> divide the spoil with the strong,
> because he exposed himself to death,
> and he was numbered with the transgressors, and he did bear the
> sin of many,
> and made intercession for the transgressors."

The only way to understand this passage is that the servant is delivered from his suffering and escapes some deadly menace. His days are prolonged, he lives to see his offspring grow; he prospers and becomes a great, mighty man. And because his knowledge, righteousness, and innocence survives suffering, his exaltation and prospering is a blow for sin and transgression, and in this way many are justified without having to go through the suffering of the servant. Therefore it was said earlier in the song that the servant bore others' griefs and sorrows (53:4) and was wounded and bruised for others' sins and transgressions and with his stripes they were healed (53:5).

The song says nothing about the resurrection of the servant, and it is hardly justified to maintain, as many Christian students do, that the resurrection is implied. It is unbelievable that any writer would imply such an extraordinary thing despite such silence. The conclusion that we should derive from the way exaltation and prospering of the servant is described is that the suffering of the servant, if he is an individual figure, never actually led to his death but simply exposed him to it. This establishes a point about which we argued earlier on other grounds. It also shows that Christian use of the song as a prediction of the vicarious death and resurrection of Jesus is not justified on the basis of the text of the song.

Moreover, such a use of the song also has no roots in the teachings of Jesus, or of the earliest church or of the synagogue. "The tradition of Jesus' sayings reveals no trace of a consciousness on his part of being the Servant of God of Is. 53," says Rudolf Bultmann in *Theology of the New Testament*, I, p. 31. And turning to the teachings of the church and the synagogue, he goes on to say:

The messianic interpretation of Is. 53 was discovered in the Christian Church, and even in it evidently not immediately. The passion story, whose telling is colored by proof of predictions, reveals the influence especially of Ps. 21 (22) and 68 (69), but not before Lk. 22:37 is there any influence from Is. 53. In Mt. 8:17, even Is. 53:4, so easily applied to vicarious suffering, serves as a prediction not of the suffering, but of the healing Messiah. The earliest passages in which the Suffering Servant of God of Is. 53 clearly and certainly appears in the *Interpretation Christiana* are: Acts 8:32f., I Pet. 2:22-25, Heb. 9:28. Such interpretations may be older than Paul and perhaps is behind Rom. 4:25, which is probably a saying quoted by Paul. Whether Is. 53 is thought of in "according to the scriptures," I Cor. 15:3, cannot be said. It is significant that

Paul himself nowhere adduces the figure of the Servant of God. The synoptic predictions of the passion obviously do not have Is. 53 in mind; otherwise why it is nowhere referred to? Only later do such specific references as I Clem. 16:3-14 and Barn 5:2 come along. So far as it understood Is. 53 messianically, the synagogue applied precisely the suffering and death of the Servant not to the Messiah, but to the People (or to something else).

In addition to the Fourth Servant Song, Christian students also apply some psalms to the suffering of Jesus. Thus, for example, referring to Ps. 22 (which is too long to be quoted here), C. A. Briggs says; "These sufferings transcend those of any historical sufferer, with the single exception of Jesus Christ. They find their exact counterpart in the sufferings of the cross . . . in the piercing of the hands and feet, the body stretched upon the cross, the intense thirst, and the division of the garments." (Matt 27:39-46, Mark 15:34, Luke 23:25-38, John 19:23-30). But in connection with any such application we must note: 1) by tracing the history of tradition from the earliest gospel to the last we can see clearly that if there are any correspondences between the sufferings of Jesus and those mentioned in the psalms, it is largely because the accounts of Jesus' passion were written decades after his death *with the psalms in mind;* 2) these psalms were never in the first place understood to refer to the suffering of any messianic figure; and 3) they can be applied with even greater justification to the suffering of other men of God, such as Prophet Muhammad (SAWS) (see below) even though the stories of such men were never told under the influence of the psalms or the Fourth Servant Song.

Nevertheless, the Old Testament passages about suffering and their Christian application have made one point: the road to noble achievements in history passes through suffering (cf. Qur'an 2:214) and even messiah-like figures must suffer to achieve the glorious things they were hoped to achieve. It can also be said that such messengers of God suffer because of the transgression of others and for the purpose that others may be saved.

Suffering of the Messianic Trinity

If, as we have argued throughout this book, messianic prophecies find their fulfillment through John, Jesus, and Muhammad (SAWS) and if suffering is an essential part of great messianic work, then it is noteworthy that not only Jesus but also John and Muhammad (AS) endured extreme suffering in their work. Most of my Christian readers know how

John was imprisoned and then beheaded for his righteousness, but they may not know how Prophet Muhammad (SAWS) and all his followers underwent the most terrible kinds of suffering for a long period of 13 years before his mission could see any signs of success. The following account of Muhammad's sufferings may therefore be quite informative for some readers.

When in 611 A.C. Muhammad (SAWS) started his mission as a messenger of God to all mankind, he was first received by his fellow citizens with curiosity and laughter, but this soon turned into an ever increasing hostility. Of the few persons who heeded the call of Muhammad (SAWS), those who did not have any powerful relatives were treated most cruelly. Slaves like Bilal and Khabbab were often made to lie on scorching desert sand or live cinders under crushing weights. Their lives were spared because they still had value as slaves, but others like the parents of Ammar bin Yasir were stabbed or beaten to death.

Muhammad himself had a powerful uncle, Abu Talib, who protected him for a while, but this protection extended only to Muhammad's life. It did not protect him from jeers, indignity, and insults. People called him mad or possessed and often yelled insulting comments as he passed by. Some of the more serious of his enemies who lived in his neighborhood used to throw garbage and other unclean and offensive things at him as he walked by their houses or as he cooked his food upon his hearth; for example, once they flung upon him the entrails of a goat. Some of those who opposed and insulted the Prophet Muhammad (SAWS) were his own relatives.

At this stage of hostility, Muhammad (SAWS) could well have said the following words from Psalm 69:7-12:

> It is for Thy sake (O Lord) that I have been insulted and shame hath covered my face.
> I have become a stranger unto my brethren and an alien unto my mother's children
> For my devotion to Thine house has eaten me up and the reproaches of those who reproach Thee are fallen on me.
> I humble myself by fasting and people insult me.
> I made sackcloth also my garment and I became a proverb to them
> They that sit in the gate speak against me; and I was the song of the drunkards.

As the Prophet Muhammad (SAWS) was being subjected to indignities and insults, attempts were made at the same time to eliminate his respected uncle's protection of his life. A couple of times a body of elders went to Abu Talib and told him how Muhammad (SAWS) was speaking against their and Abu Talib's gods and ancestral religion and how he called them ignorant and their forefathers misled. Then they asked him to leave Muhammad (SAWS) "to us that we may take our satisfaction." When such persuasion failed, the elders resorted to much harsher measures. In the seventh year of the mission, a ban was imposed on the clan of Abu Talib, including, of course, Muhammad (SAWS) and his family. According to this ban, the citizens "would not marry the women (of Abu Talib's clan), nor give their own in marriage to them; they would sell nothing to them, nor buy aught from them; in short, dealings of every kind should cease." These terms of the decision were committed to writing, sealed with three seals, and hung up in the Ka'ba, thus giving religious sanction to the hostility of all Makka towards one man, who had but a handful of followers and friends and whose only fault was to preach the worship, not of idols, but of the one true living God, Allah (SWT).

The ban was rigorously put into force. The isolated group was forced to withdraw to a secluded defile in a mountain on the eastern outskirts of the city. They soon found themselves cut off from supplies of food and other necessities of life. They were not strong enough to send forth a caravan of their own; if foreign merchants came, they were made to withhold their commodities except at an exorbitant price; (Makkans) themselves would sell them nothing; and a great scarcity followed. "The citizens could hear the wailing of the famished children" (William Muir, The Life of Mahomet, p. 94). The survival of the band was ensured only by outside sympathizers who would bring in provisions secretly from time to time at night.

When the ban was lifted after two years, it did not for long reduce the sufferings of Muhammad (SAWS). Soon after the lifting of the ban, and probably because of the hardships suffered during it, Muhammad (SAWS) had to face in quick succession the deaths of both his uncle and his dear wife, Khadija - the two persons after Allah that served as his sources of external and internal security. His reaction to these losses was deeply emotional: grief and tears.

With Abu Talib gone, people took even greater liberties in subjecting Muhammad (SAWS) to insult and injury. Thorns were laid in his path and the populace would cast dust upon his head. On one occasion he returned home with his head covered with dust and one of his daughters rose, with tears in her eyes, to wipe it off. Muhammad (SAWS) comforted her, saying: "My daughter, weep not, for verily the Lord will be thy father's helper."

Once the city populace tried to inflict a different kind of injury on the Prophet (SAWS). He went out one day, and not one of the people looked at him or spoke to him or even injured him and this hurt the Prophet (SAWS) most of all. The situation of the Prophet (SAWS) in the city at this stage may roughly be depicted by the following passages from the Bible:

I am like a pelican of the wilderness
I am like an owl of the desert
I watch and am as a sparrow alone upon the house top.
Mine enemies reproach me all the day and they that are mad against me are sworn against me. (Ps. 102:6-8)

For my love they are my adversaries: but I give myself to prayer. And they have rewarded me evil for good and hatred for my love. (Ps. 109:4-5)

All the time that the Prophet (SAWS) was enduring all this suffering he was, of course, taking every opportunity to preach his message, namely, that man should not worship anything or anybody except the one true living God, Allah, the Lord and Creator of the universe, and that man is accountable for his actions. When he was under ban in the outskirts of the city he concentrated on his relatives, but at other times he would address whoever would listen to him. At the annual pilgrimage, he would preach to the numerous visitors from outside Makka. But his efforts among the pilgrims were frustrated by Abu Lahab, who would follow the Prophet (SAWS) everywhere and cry aloud: "Believe him not, he is a lying renegade!" And the Prophet, grieved and troubled, would look upward and say, "O Lord, if Thou willest, it would not be thus!"

In the year 620 A.C. the Prophet decided to personally take his mission outside Makka. The city of Al-Taif was the natural first choice; situated about sixty miles east of Makka, it was the nearest city of importance. Accompanied only by Zayd, his ex-slave and adopted son, Muhammad (SAWS) travelled to Al-Taif through barren defiles over dismal fields of boulders. During the ten days he spent in Al-Taif, he preached to many influential men as well as to common people. But they all rejected his message because they did not want to depart radically from their traditional religion and to take the risk that was involved in following him. They not only rejected his message, but also turned hostile towards him.

"Stirred up to hasten the departure of the unwelcome visitor, the people hooted him through the streets, pelted him with stones, and at last obliged him to flee the city, pursued by a relentless rabble. Blood flowed from both his legs; and Zayd, endeavoring to shield him, was wounded in the head. The mob did not desist until they had chased him two or three miles across the sandy plain to the foot of the surrounding hills. There, wearied and mortified, he took refuge in one of the numerous orchards, and rested under a vine."(William Muir, op.cit., p. 109)

The turning point in the Prophet's mission came when on the hill of Aqaba one day he met six men just arriving for pilgrimage from Yathrib (later called Medina). The Prophet (SAWS) sat with the travellers and preached his message to them at length. When he had finished, the men forthwith embraced Islam. More than that, upon their return they started an Islamic mission in Medina which gradually prospered to such an extent that Muhammad (SAWS) could not only be safe there, but welcome. At this stage, the Prophet (SAWS) instructed his followers in Makka secretly to migrate to Medina as soon as they could, and so within a few months most of the believers (about 150) were able to find a new and safer home. But the Prophet's own person was still in deadly danger.

Just when the preparation for the arrival of the Prophet Muhammad (SAWS) in Medina was complete and he was ready to leave his beloved Makka, the elders of the city realized what it might mean for their prestigious religious position in the Arabian Peninsula if Muhammad (SAWS) could readily preach a radically new religion from a safe and receptive Medina. They hurriedly got together at evening time to discuss what could be done before Muhammad (SAWS) himself left the city. Some suggested that he should be expelled from the country; others said that he should be detained indefinitely; still others proposed that he should be killed. The pros and cons of each action were considered, but the discussion was cut short because the time was running out. Whatever they were going to do, the first step was to take Muhammad (SAWS) into custody. Abu Jahl formed a group of strong men chosen form various families in order to distribute the blame for any violent action. He sent them to capture the Prophet Muhammad (SAWS) dead or alive. It was night time and the men expected their victim to be in his bed sleeping. So they came to Muhammad's house.

At this time, apart from some helpless slaves and 'Ali, a youth of twenty, the only followers of Muhammad (SAWS) left in Makka were Abu Bakr and his family. 'Ali was in Muhammad's house when Abu Jahl's men came. Satisfying themselves that the man they wanted was inside, they stood guard around the house. Thus, almost alone in a whole city of enemies, some of whom were surrounding his house the Prophet's situation recalls the following passages from the psalms of suffering:

> Many enemies surround me like bulls
> They have beset me round like fierce bulls of Bashan.
> They gaped upon me with their mouths, as a ravening and a roaring lion. (Ps. 22:12-13)

> Those that hate me without cause are more than the hairs of mine head;
> They that would kill me, being mine enemies wrongfully, are mighty. (Ps. 69:4)

But just like the sufferers of the psalms and of the Fourth Servant Song, who suffered for the sake of righteousness, humanity, and the glorification of God (Ps 22:22-31, Is 53:10-12), the Prophet Muhammad (SAWS), too, was delivered from the hands of this enemies to be exalted as few other men have been. By his prophetic insight, Muhammad (SAWS) knew what was going on. He waited for the late hours of the night, then quietly got up, threw his own red mantle on 'Ali, and slipped out of the house. The men outside were all asleep!

The Prophet (SAWS) went straight to Abu Bakr (RA), who had lately been making some preparation for their joint departure to Medina. After a few last-minute preparations, the two slipped out of a small back door of Abu Bakr's house and escaped unobserved from the southern end of the city. Walking on rugged rocky paths for about an hour and a half, they came at last to the peak of mount Thawr and there they took refuge in a cave. By now the day had fully dawned and they knew that Abu Jahl's men would have discovered the escape of Muhammad (SAWS) and started to search for him.

When the news of Muhammad's escape spread among the Makkan's it set the city in a ferment. Abu Jahl's men had already made inquiries from 'Ali and Abu Bakr's family, but without obtaining any useful information. Now they sent small parties of men in all directions to track down the most important fugitive in history. One party came dangerously close to the cave of Thawr where the two men were hiding. Abu Bakr became worried, but his companion said to him, "Be not cast down, for verily Allah is with us." (Qur'an 9:40) The two spent three days in the cave, supplied secretly with food by the family of Abu Bakr (RA). On the third night, when the Makkans had come to accept the Prophet's successful escape, Abu Bark's family sent a hired guide with two camels and suitable provisions for a journey to Medina and instructed him to wander about near the summit of mount Thawr. The guide and the camels were spotted by the two men and thus started a three day historic journey to freedom and to success. The two travellers arrived in Medina on 23rd June, 622, to an enthusiastic welcome. Thirteen years of persecution and suffering were over. For the next ten years the fate of the Prophet's mission was decided on battlefields and the struggle finally led to the peaceful conquest of Makkah, from which all idols were removed and where the worship of the one transcendent God, Allah (SAWS), was restored as in the days of the Prophet Abraham (AS).

The story of Muhammad's life parallels that of the suffering servant of Is. 53, if due allowance is made for the dramatic and poetic element in the song. Like the servant, Muhammad (SAWS) was at first rejected and persecuted as a transgressor. He was insulted as a mad or lying renegade, cut off from society, stoned, and exposed to death. But despite all the hostility, persecution, and dangers to his life, his days were prolonged, and he and his seed prospered (v. 10); he lived to see the success of his mission for which he travailed (v. 11). He was given in his lifetime "a portion among the great" and he divided "the spoil with the strong" (v. 12). By his knowledge he justified many (v. 11). The question of explaining Muhammad's suffering never arose with the urgency experienced by the Church in dealing with Jesus' suffering and therefore no elaborate theology developed to explain it. But one can say nevertheless that the Prophet Muhammad (SAWS) suffered on account of others' sins and for the purpose of saving others (v. 12).

To conclude this essay on the suffering of messianic figures the main points may be summarized as follows:

1) The Old Testament passages about suffering have no value as predictions of Jesus' suffering, since these passages are not meant to be predictions and many important details are not applicable to Jesus. Furthermore, one could apply these passages to Prophet Muhammad (SAWS) with much greater justification than to Jesus.

2) The Passages about suffering and their Christian application, even though this application is not justified, have served to emphasize one important point: the road to achievement of noble goals, above all messianic goals, passes through suffering. This suffering is not due to any fault of the sufferers but due to the sinfulness of others. They undergo this suffering to benefit humanity at large, and

3)   If one can speak at all of a messianic fulfillment of the Old Testament Passages about suffering, then such a fulfillment has taken place in the fact that each person in the messianic trinity - John, Jesus, and Muhammad (AS) suffered greatly at the hands of sinful men and for the sake of benefiting or saving mankind.

A Partial Survey of Muslim Science

T he purpose of this survey is to give a very rough idea of the scope of Muslim science. It has been thought useful because a great many readers of this book in the West may be quite unaware of the history of science through the Middle Ages, a history whose correct evaluation is essential for appreciating the main argument of Chapter V.

Needless to say, our survey is very far from complete. As stated earlier, most of the Muslim works have been lost to us, having been destroyed by Christians, Mongols, and anti-intellectual "Muslims." We possess long biographies of scholars and scientists such as those of Muhammad al-Tusi (d.1067), but we cannot find the overwhelming majority of the books mentioned in them. Many of the works we do possess have not yet been fully studied. The extraordinary find in 1924 in one of these texts that the lesser circulation of the blood, the discovery of which was earlier ascribed to Servetus and Columbo, was in fact discovered centuries earlier by Ibn al-Nafis, shows that even the existing texts may have many surprises in store for us.

The emphasis in this survey is on the original achievements of the Muslims, but this is not to underestimate the Muslim contribution in preserving, systematizing, and popularizing the works of earlier civilizations, a contribution which was not only necessary for the development of modern science, but has also provided valuable material for the modern historian. Many Greek works (e.g. the three books of the *Conics* of Appollonius, the *Spherics* of Menelaus, the *Mechanics* of Hero of Alexandria, the *Pneumatics* of Philo of Byzantium, a short book on the balance attributed to Euclid, and a work on the elepsydra ascribed to Archimides) are to be found today only in Muslim translations.

We may begin our survey with the earth sciences. Beginning with the Abbasid period, Muslim geographers had collected a vast amount of data about various lands (including a land of the Zenjis where the day lasts only six hours - South Australia?) and made much more exact computations of longitude and latitude than those made by their predecessors. By the fourteenth century (1331 A.C.) we find Muslim geographers composing or helping to compose the official Chinese map (A.Z. Validi, "Islam and the Science of Geography", *Islamic Culture*, October 1934, p. 514), and by the early sixteenth century we find Ibn Majid guiding the voyages of Vasco de Gama and Pir Muhyi al-Din Ra'is producing maps of Africa and America that continue to astonish modern scholars (S.H. Nasr, *Islamic Sciences*, London, 1976, pp. 44-45).

Muslim geographers enriched their works more extensively than did their predecessors with anecdotes, descriptions of natural scenic beauty, etc., and assigned greater value to civic and cultural life, language, beliefs, and manners. As a result, Muslim geographical works still retain great value as sources for the histories of various nations.

Just before the advent of the European renaissance, Muslims made notable advances in nautical geography. The influence of works of this period in the West is reflected in such meteorological terms as typhoon (from the Arabic *tufan*) and monsoon (from *mawsim*).

Al-Biruni, who devoted about fifteen books to geodesy and mathematical geography, is considered the founder of geodesy (S.H. Barani, "Muslim Researches in Geodesy," *Islamic Culture*, Vol. 6, 1932, pp. 363-369). In the 13th century, Abu'l-'Ali al Marrakushi wrote works that are described by Sarton as "the most important contributions to mathematical geography - not only in Islam but anywhere." (G.Sarton, *An Introduction to the History of Science.*)

"It is surprising to realize how many geological observations and ideas which came to be substantiated during later centuries were already known to Muslims." Their writings on geology "show a clear understanding of the gradual character of geological change, of the major transformations which have taken place on the surface of the earth, including the changing of lands into sea and of sea into land, of the importance at the same time of many cataclysms such as violent earthquakes, which have transformed the sculpture of the surface of the earth, and of the importance of rocks as a record of the earth's geological history." (S.H.Nasr, op. cit., p.51). Concerning the importance of records contained in rocks, al-Biruni, one of the foremost Muslim geologists, writes: "We have to rely upon the records of rocks and vestiges of the past to infer that all these changes should have taken place in very, very long times and under unknown conditions of cold and heat." (Z. Validi Togan, *Biruni's Picture of the World, Memoirs of the Archaelogical Survey of India*, Vol. 53, Calcutta, 1937-1938, pp. 57-58). Al-Biruni also makes the most remarkable observation that the Ganges Plain in India is sedimentary deposit: "One of these plains is India, limited in the South by the above-mentioned Indian Ocean, and on three sides by lofty mountains, the waters of which flow down to it. But if you see the soil of India with your own eyes and meditate on its nature, if you consider the rounded stones found in the earth however deeply you dig, stones that are huge near the mountains and where the rivers are violent currents, stones that are of smaller size at a greater distance from the mountains and where the streams flow more slowly, stones that appear pulverized in the shape of sand where the streams begin to stagnate near their mouths and near the sea - if you consider all this, you can scarcely help thinking that India was once a sea, which by degrees had been filled up by the alluvium of streams." (*Albiruni's India*, trans. by E.E. Sachau, London, 1910, Vol. I, p. 198).

"Muslim students of geology were also fully aware of the origin of fossils. Usually in Western histories of geology and paleontology it is mentioned that after millennia of confusion concerning the origin of fossils, suddenly in (the 18th) century a clear scientific explanation was provided. Actually nothing could be further from the truth if Islamic sources are taken into account. The *Epistles* of the Brethren of Purity written in the 10th century had already described fossils as remains of sea animals which had become petrified in a place which is now land but which had been a sea in bygone ages." (S.H. Nasr, op. cit., p. 52)

Islamic thinkers devoted attention to various theories of evolution. Al-Nazzam (first half of the ninth century) explained the theory of an enfoldment of hidden creation. The essential point of this doctrine is that creation was complete at the outset although only part of it appears at a time. According to Sarton, "This is truly a theory of evolution, and the word *evolution* was first used by Charles Bonet about 1762 with that very acceptation." (Op.cit., p. 61). A Persian work, twelfth century, entitled *Four Discourses*, tells of attempts to identify 'missing links'; it describes coral as intermediate between the mineral and vegetable kingdoms; the vine which seeks to avoid and escape from the fatal embrace of a kind of bindweed called *'ashaqa* as intermediate between the vegetable and animal kingdoms; and *nasnas*, a kind of ape or wild man, as intermediate between the animal and human kingdom. (Edward G. Bresone, Arabian Medicine, p. 118-119; Robert Gulick, *Muhammad; The Educator*, Lahore, p. 106).

In mathematics Muslims developed a comprehensive system of reckoning based on the Indian numerals and established it not only in the Islamic lands but also in the West, bringing about a transformation which influenced nearly all aspects of life and thought from pure mathematics to commerce and trade" (S.H. Nasr, op. cit., p. 79). Among the legacies of this heritage all such terms of Arabic origin as *algorithm* in English and *guarismo* in Spanish (from the name *Al-Khawarizmi* of the Persian mathematician, whose books were the first on arithmetic to be translated into European languages) and cipher (from the Arabic *sifr* for zero). Trigonometry, even as it is studied now, was developed almost completely by Muslim mathematicians. They were the first to formulate the trigonometric functions explicitly - indeed the word 'sine' is the direct translation of the Arabic word *jayb* (see A. I. Sabra, "ilm al-hisab" in the *Encyclopaedia of Islam*) and to discover many trigonometric formulas such as $2 \cos a \cos b = \cos (a+b) + \cos (a-b)$, $2 \sin 2/a/2 = 1 - \cos a$. They were also the first to demonstrate the sine theorem for a general spherical triangle.

Algebra, too, was entirely a Muslim addition to mathematics. It started seriously with a book by Al-Khawarizmi whose Arabic title, in fact, gave the science its title. From the 10th to the 14th century we find Muslim mathematicians solving equations with up to five unknowns; or cubic equations like $x^3 + a = cx^2$ that arise in Archimides' problem of cutting a sphere by a plane so that the two parts are in a given proportion to each other. We find them proving that $x^3 + y^3 = z^3$ has no solution in whole numbers, which must have been extended by Fermat as his famous unproven proposition. The famous Persian poet Omar Khayyam (died in 1132 A.C.) classified algebraic equations up to the third degree in a systematic way and solved them by geometric methods (see W.E. Story, *Omar As a Mathematician*, Boston, 1918). Al-Kharaji provided a basis for most of Fibonacci's works (see F. Wiepecke, *Extrait du fakhri*, Paris, 1853).

Al-Karkhi's work contains the first treatment of indeterminate equations (Gaston Wiet et al, *The Medieval Civilization*, London, P. 648).

Another Muslim mathematician, Al-Kashani, solved the binomial known by the name of Newton, inverted the decimal fractions, discovered the approximate method for calculating problems that have no exact solution, and the iterative algorithm, and made a remarkably accurate calculation of π. He must also be considered the first person to have invented a calculating machine (E. S. Kennedy, *A Fifteenth*

Century Planetary Computer, al-Kashani's Tabaq Al-Manatig, Isis, vol. 41, 1950, pp. 180-183; Vol. 43, 1952, pp. 42-50).

Muslim mathematicians also studied numerical series, knew how to sum finite series like $1 + 2 + 2^2 + \ldots\ldots 2^n$, studied continued fractions and thereby discovered irrational numbers. They also developed techniques of computation far beyond what had existed before so that they were able, for example, to attain a precision of one in ten million for the table of trigonometric tangent function.

In geometry, Banu Musa, the three enterprising sons of Musa ibn Shakir, found the structure of the ellipse with a chord fixed at the two foci, and also worked on the trisection of an angle. Banu Musa had a taste for the mechanical and they set themselves practical problems, connected with spurting fountains, and with an apparatus for collecting pearls from the sea-bed.

Thabit ibn Qurra wrote a treatise on the conclusiveness of proof by algebraic calculation and his grandson, Ibrahim ibn Simam, perfected the procedure of Archimedes for squaring the parabola and devised a method not improved upon until the advent of the integral calculus, which method contains something of its main idea.

Omar Khayyam and Tusi made observations that could be followed by the development of non-Euclidean geometry (S.H. Nasr, op. cit.)

The way several Muslim mathematicians related problems in algebra and geometry clearly makes them originators of analytic geometry.

Al-Kindi (died 873 A.C.) realized the importance of mathematics for science and wrote a book entitled *The Impossibility of an Understanding of Philosophy without Mathematics.* Philosophy, it should be noted, signified for past scholars, science and learning in general. Evidently this realization of the importance of mathematics for science was to some extent shared with al-Kindi by many other Muslim scientists, since we find them making extensive applications of mathematics to various sciences.

In astronomy we find Muslims inventing many instruments for their astronomical observations. Khujani determined the inclination of the ecliptic with the aid of a sextant of his own invention. Saghani, a persian from Merv, also invented many instruments for his research (Gaston Wiet et al, op. cit., p 648). Al-Biruni invented the orthographical astrolabe. Abul Hasan invented the telescope, of which he speaks as "a tube to the extremities of which were attached diopters" (see Amir Ali, *The Spirit of Islam, p. 345).* Muslims were the first to establish observatories as scientific institutions as they are understood today (S.H. Nasr, op. cit., pp 112-126). It was Farghani who first wrote a study of sundials (Gaston Wiet et al, op. cit., p. 644).

The first notable feature of Islamic astronomy is of course the vast amount of actual observation that was made of the heavens, far more than was undertaken by the Greeks. Old constants were improved and new star catalogues composed; many new stars (many of which still bear Arabic names in European languages) were discovered, the inclination of the ecliptic was remeasured, and the motion of the solar apogee was observed and tied to the movement of the fixed stars (S. H. Nasr, op.cit., pp. 131-132). Nasr al Din Al-Tusi and his associates at the observatory of Maraghah gave new planetary theories that were used by Copernicus and later European astronomers. They also discussed the possibility of the earth's rotation. One of them, Qutb al Din al-Shirazi, formulated the first satisfactory theory of the rainbow (Sarton, op. cit., p. 22).

"Another important feature of Islamic astronomy was the new method of applying mathematics to astronomy. As already mentioned, Muslim scientists used the calculus of sines and trigonometry instead of the calculus of chords and were therefore able to achieve much greater precision in their measurements. They also perfected computation techniques dealing with the motion of the planets far beyond anything achieved before." (S. H. Nasr, op. cit., p. 132).

The following words of al-Biruni are worthy of records as an indication of the scientific independence and objectivity with which some Muslim scientists handled data: "Rotation of the earth would in no way invalidate astronomical calculations, for all the astronomical data are as explicable in terms of the one theory as of the other. The problem is thus difficult of solution." (Quoted from Gaston Wiet et al, op. cit., p. 649).

We turn to physics by noting that Galileo based some of his views on those of the Andalusian philosopher Ibn Bajjah (the Latin Avempace). (See E. A. Moody, Galileo and Avempace, *"Journal of the History of Ideas,* Vol. XII, No. 2, 1951, pp. 163-193; No. 3, 1951, pp. 375-422). Muslims developed such cardinal concepts as momentum and made extensive studies of gravity. They knew that acceleration of a body falling under gravity did not depend on its mass and also that the power of attraction between two bodies increased as their distance decreased and as their mass increased (See Jalal Shawq, *Arab Heritage in Mechanics* (Arabic), Cairo, 1973, p. 51, 75-78).

In optics Muslim contributions are relatively better known, thanks to the works of Ibn al-Haytham (the west's Alhazen), which influenced not only earlier European students such as Witelo, Roger Bacon, and Peckham, but also Kepler and Newton. Ibn al-Haytham knew a great deal of the anatomy of the eye and the role of its various parts in vision. At the very least he knew, with several other Muslim scientists whose views he collected and developed, that rays of light do not issue from the eye but that during the process of vision rays of light reach the eye from the object in sight. Ibn al-Haytham concentrated a great deal of his efforts in the study of parabolic and spherical mirrors and their aberrations. He raised and solved the problem known to this day by his name: given a spherical mirror and an object with its image, find the point of reflection. His solution involved solving a fourth degree equation by geometric means. Ibn al-Haytham was the first to demonstrate the second law of reflection, namely that the incident ray, the normal, and the reflected ray are in the same plane. He also made many significant discoveries about refraction. He discovered that a ray of light takes the easier and quicker path, a thesis which enunciates the principle of "least time" associated with the name of Fermat. He also applied the rectangle of velocities at the surface of refraction long before Newton.

Ibn al-Haytham also made many studies of great astronomical and meteorological significance. He determined the thickness of the atmosphere, the effect of the atmosphere on the observation of celestial phenomena, the beginning and end of twilight, the reason why the sun and the moon are larger on the horizon than in the middle of the sky, and many other optical phenomena.

Ibn al-Haytham was a great experimentalist. He made numerous experiments with glass cylinders immersed in water to study refraction and also sought to determine the magnifying power of lenses. He devised a lathe with the help of which he made lenses for his experiments. He studied the *Camera Obscura* mathematically for the first time and made an experiment that also for the first time made possible the experimental demonstration that light travels in a straight line. He was able to plan experiments carefully and at the same time analyze problems mathematically, (S. H. Nasr, op. cit., pp. 141-142).

Al-Khazini was aware of the role of heat in affecting the density of objects.

Farabi, as a remarkable theorist of music, made possible some advances in the theory of the physical basis of sound, notably on the question of the spherical propagation of sound (Gaston Wiet et al, op. cit., p. 647).

Muslim science was aware of the phenomenon of magnetism (Ibid, pp. 662-665).

Al-Kindi, who also wrote on tides, on the iron and steel of weapons and on the theory of music, has left an opuscule on compound medicines. The work has been "recently studied by L. Gauthier, who was surprised to find that it contained in embryo the principles of modern psychophysics. Speaking of medicinal doses and their effect on maladies, Kindi makes what is essentially a statement of the law of the correspondence of the geometric progression of stimuli and arithmetic progression of sensations." (Gaston Wiet et al, op. cit., p. 645).

Al-Razi (the West's Rhazes) left more than 200 books on medicine, natural science, alchemy, mathematics, optics, astronomy, theology, and philosophy. some of these works were, of course, short monographs but one of them, *Kitab al-Hasani,* was so voluminous that when translated in Europe it was, at first, mistaken as prepared by his disciples from his collected papers. A work of importance by al-Razi is his treatise on smallpox and measles, which is the oldest reliable account of these diseases, having no greek counterpart. (Ibid, p. 653). Razi also made a study of alchemy, but departed from the well-trodden path of mysticism and symbolism to give precise methods of technical experiments, with a detailed description of substances and instruments. It may be said that it was he who laid the basis of scientific chemistry. (Ibid, p.653). Al-Razi gave the first theological formulation of faith in a continuous scientific advance, with emphasis on the provisional nature of all research whose conclusions can be revised at all times.

'Ali Majusti was the first to attempt a comprehensive and methodical presentation of medicine as a whole. He may be called the father of the medical "intern" system, for he required that the student be present at the professor's examination of patients. Edward Brown has shown how Ali propounded in a rudimentary form the theory of the system of capillary vessels.

Ammar ibn 'Ali probably invented the resorption operation for cataract.

Ibn Sina (the West's Avicenna) was an infant prodigy - at eighteen he was reputed to be an excellent doctor and at twenty-one he began to write books. His *Cannon of Medicine* is perhaps the most influential single work in the whole history of medicine. Besides making extensive use of all the medical experience and knowledge of earlier Islamic and non-Islamic sources available to him, Ibn Sina made many new observations of his own, including the discovery of meningitis, the manner of spread of epidemics, the contagious nature of tuberculosis, etc. He also made many discoveries in what is today called psychosomatic medicine (S. H. Nasr, op. cit., pp. 178-179).

The Andalusian physician, Abu Marwan ibn Zuhr, produced in the 12th century the first scientific work on diet ever composed, *The Book of Diet*.

Muslims developed numerous surgical instruments, the knowledge of which reached the West through the work, *The Book of Concession*, by Abu'l Qasim al-Zahrawi, well-known to Europe as Albucasis. They also developed such great skill in the external, non-surgical, treatment of broken or dislocated parts of the body that its practitioners are able to compete successfully even with modern physicians.

Ala al-din ibn Nafis, centuries before Servetus and Columbo, had correctly explained the minor circulation of the blood (see Meyerhoff, "Ibn al-Nafis, XIIth century) and his Theory of Lesser Circulation," *ISIS*, Vol. 23, 1935, pp. 100-120). What makes the discovery by al-Nafis all the more remarkable is that he arrived at it without any dissection.

Ibn al-Quff, a student of Ibn al-Nafis, was the first person to have pointed out clearly the existence of capillaries which were seen under a microscope for the first time by Malpighi in 1661. Shams al-Din al-Akfani wrote the first work on first aid entitled, *The Refuge of the Intelligent During the Absence of the Physician*.

In technology Muslims invented a variety of instruments for their experiments and measurements and a number of gadgets of varying degrees of complexity for amusement and other more practical purposes. In some lands like Persia the Muslims developed amazing irrigation systems, for some of which a remarkable degree of mathematical ingenuity was used (S. H. Nasr, op. cit., p. 217).

In agriculture Muslims transferred numerous plants from one region of the earth to another and improved stocks through grafting and the like. "The spread of such products as coffee (from the Arabic *Qahwah)* seville oranges, cotton, sugar cane, various kinds of melons, peaches, and artichokes (from the Arabic *al-kharshuf),* to cite but a few examples, not only from one part of the Islamic world to another but also to Europe and ultimately to America attest to the world-wide influence of agricultural activity by Muslims. In such regions as Andalusia the Muslims transformed whole patterns of agriculture. . ." (Nasr, 218).